Foreign and Comparative Studies/African Series XXVI

Linguistic Diversity and Language Belief in Kenya: The Special Position of Swahili

by John Rhoades

Maxwell
School of Citizenship
and Public Affairs
Syracuse University

For two decades the Maxwell School has had as a major thrust of its teaching and research programs a concentration upon the world outside our national borders. In 1975 this commitment to foreign and comparative studies stands as a *sine qua non* of our intellectual endeavors. Increasingly the scholar and teacher is obliged to consider the influences on his work from outside our borders in order to diminish the culture-bound nature of the social sciences.

Maxwell's organization for teaching and research purposes emphasized discrete areas of the world: Soviet and East Europe, Latin America, Eastern Africa and South Asia. In addition, numerous faculty members have come here with interests in Western European countries and subjects. During the fifties and sixties, grants to subsidize a variety of such programs and interests came abundantly to Maxwell as to many other universities. That day is now gone – in fact, the scarcity of funds for supporting teaching and research about the rest of the world is a disturbing reality. As the pressures for neo-isolationism grow, as the energy shortage and related "crises" unfold, the university should feel even more sharply its extra-national role.

The Foreign and Comparative Studies Program is the present expression of Maxwell's awareness of the imperative for attention to foreign and international questions. This Program coordinates and supervises undergraduate and graduate concentrations which involve comparative and area studies. It encourages and motivates faculty cooperation in inter-regional research and teaching more effectively to meet the demands and opportunities of the present day.

The Foreign and Comparative Studies Monograph Series is a central part of this enterprise. It subsumes the series previously published by the Eastern African Studies Program and envisions an expansion of the output from the Latin American, South Asian, Soviet and East European and Western European faculties. Today, Maxwell has a large number of faculty members whose research interests include these areas. This series is a medium for their publishing manuscripts scheduled to appear in standard journals at a later date, monographs too long to appear in journals and yet not of book length, and other items. Scholars elsewhere are invited to submit their manuscripts for consideration for publication as parts of the series.

Publishing Desk
211 Maxwell School
Syracuse University
Syracuse, New York 13210
USA

LINGUISTIC DIVERSITY AND LANGUAGE BELIEF IN KENYA:
THE SPECIAL POSITION OF SWAHILI

by

John Rhoades

FOREIGN AND COMPARATIVE STUDIES/AFRICAN SERIES XXVI

Maxwell School of Citizenship and Public Affairs

Syracuse University

1977

Library of Congress Cataloging in Publication Data
Rhoades, John. Linguistic Diversity and Language Belief in Kenya.
Foreign and Comparative Studies: African Series: 26
1. Swahili Language in Kenya.
2. Swahili wit and humor--Kenya--history and criticism.
3. Kenyan wit and humor--history and criticism.
I. Title., II. Series.
PL8701.R5 496'.392 77-20016
ISBN 0-915984-23-7

TABLE OF CONTENTS

PREFACE

This study is an attempt to investigate popular stereotypes about the use of Swahili in Kenya. The data are reader-contributed jokes written for the Swahili language newspaper Baraza.

In 1971, when I was studying Swahili at Syracuse University as a doctoral student in anthropology, I came across Baraza in the library of the Program of Eastern African Studies. I was searching for interesting contemporary Swahili reading materials and the Cheka na Baraza (Laugh with Baraza) columns in particular seemed to supply entertainment as well. As I (humorlessly) wrestled with translating them, however, it became apparent that the jokes with their depictions of speech marked by non-Standard Swahili, English words, and current slang not to be found in the Standard Swahili-English Dictionary (published in 1939)--were a form of popular literature which offered a unique look at stereotypes about Swahili.

There is more than entertainment in looking at these stereotypes. The term "Swahili" refers to a variety of linguistic forms: the dialects spoken as first languages along the coast, the Standard form chosen as the national language for Tanzania and Kenya, and the many attenuated or pidgin second language forms commonly used as lingua franca throughout eastern Africa. This diversity in structure and function can be understood only partly by linguistic comparisons. In Kenya alone Swahili may be as much an object of social, scientific, and political concern and manipulation as it is a means of communication. Of the many social forces that are shaping the functional position of Swahili in Kenya today, popular beliefs about its use are among the most important, but unfortunately also the least studied. Because it is a second language to most Kenyans, Swahili's development cannot rest upon the implicit language loyalty which speakers usually give to their first or mother tongue language. Swahili is Kenya's national language, but this was done by government action as part of a deliberate effort to build national identity rather than by a groundswell of popular sentiment based upon an existing identity with Swahili. I am not suggesting that Swahili should not be Kenya's national language nor that it is unable to function effectively in this capacity. I am suggesting that the opinions that Kenyans have about Swahili will affect the way that it will be used and so therefore the content of popular beliefs should be studied and analyzed. This information will be of value not only to language planners in Kenya but also will contribute to a better understanding of the process by which second languages are functionally altered and symbolically transformed into national languages.

My research in Kenya was supported in part by an NDEA Title VI Foreign Language Fellowship. I am grateful to the editor of Baraza, Francis Khamisi, for allowing me access to the Cheka na Baraza jokes. During the time I conducted by research in Kenya, I was attached to the Department of Sociology at the University of Nairobi as a research associate and I wish to thank its chairman, Kivutu Ndeti, and, subsequently, Phillip Mbithi, for their assistance. Carol Scotton, then of the Department of Linguistics at the University of Nairobi, supplied helpful criticism and counsel during the early stages of the research. Iddi Abdallah, Rachel Angogo, William Frank, Muturi Gachuhi, Stephen Muhia, and Francis Tendwa all assisted in a number of important ways with data collection. The final stages of analysis and writing benefited from the contructive criticism and advice of Agehananda Bharati, Hans Buechler and Marshall Segall of Syracuse University. I am especially indebted to my dissertation adviser, Susan S. Wadley, who conscientiously supplied criticism, guidance and invaluable encouragement.

John Rhoades
Rochester, 1977

INTRODUCTION

This study is an investigation into the social significance of Swahili language varieties in Kenya. In particular, it is a study of stereotypes concerning the position of Swahili as a second language. The primary data for this study are jokes taken from a reader-contributed joke column--called Cheka na Baraza ("Laugh with Baraza")--in the Nairobi-based Swahili weekly newspaper Baraza. These jokes (singular: kichekesho, plural: vichekesho), with few exceptions, are written in the form of a conversation between two, or more, characters. Typically after a brief introduction to the situation, the body of the joke is presented as a dialogue with each character speaking in turn. In short, these jokes are depictions of speech behavior. Their content, especially the way speech is depicted and the way speech misunderstandings are related to Swahili, can provide a suitable vehicle for investigating beliefs about language use.

The fact that the jokes appear in Baraza is as important as their form. Baraza is one of the major Kenyan newspapers with a current weekly circulation of 60,000. It has a national and East African focus--its news accounts are primarily about national and regional affairs. Moreover, half the newspaper contains reader-contributed material which also reflect a national focus. Because the newspaper has this broad orientation, and because it is in Swahili, which is a second language to most of the readers, the Cheka na Baraza jokes can be assumed to be topically oriented toward general interest. They should be understood by a wide audience and consequently reflect national social beliefs and stereotypes.

Swahili is spoken as a mother-tongue by relatively few Kenyans. The Waswahili, or Swahili speakers, in general, are clustered mainly in the coastal cities. In 1969, according to the Kenya census, they were less than one percent of the total population and they do not constitute a dominant social or political group. Swahili is not an important language because it is the mother-tongue of an important people; its importance is in its wide use as a second language (a lingua franca) of inter-ethnic and official affairs.

Swahili was generally supported as a territorial lingua franca by the British during the colonial period, and largely because of this, today is an official language of Kenya (together with English). It is used in most areas of national affairs, although there are domains, such as secondary school and college instruction, where at present only English is used.

Very generally, Kenya has what Nida and Wonderly (1971) call a typical "three-language structure" consisting of the "In-group languages" (the local vernaculars), an "Out-group language" (Swahili), and a "Language of Specialized Information" (English). As in-group languages, the local vernaculars function as a means of communicating the "basic face-to-face relationships with other speakers with whom the individual in question fully identifies" (Nida and Wonderly 1971:57-58). The language of specialized information--English--is, on the other hand primarily used as a medium for communications about Western forms of technology and social-political affairs. The out-group language, Swahili, falls somewhat between these two language types. It is widely used in the marketplace and in the urban areas for communication between speakers of different vernaculars. But Swahili's position is changing; it is partially replacing English as a language of education, and it is used equally with English in the various media, especially radio.

A description of the use of Swahili in relation to English and the vernaculars only partially describes its position in Kenya. Swahili (and each of the other languages) is also an object of beliefs concerning its value as a means of communication and identity. One significant belief concerning Swahili involves its suitability as a symbol of Kenyan nationalism. This belief is manifested in the following excerpt from a letter printed in the Swahili-language newspaper Taifa (Nairobi May 23, 1970) entitled "Kiswahili ndiyo lugha ya Taifa la Kenya" (Swahili is indeed the language of the nation of Kenya):

> Mwananchi anayependelea Kiingereza zaidi ya Kiswahili inafaa asafiri hadi Uingereza. . .

> (A citizen who prefers English over Swahili should go to England. . .) (author's translation)

The writer of this letter is writing in support of a KANU (Kenya African National Union) declaration that Swahili should become Kenya's national language. In addition to his support, the writer also expresses the view that Kenyans who do not support Swahili over English are not proper Kenyans (the writer refers to them as wazungu weusi, black Europeans). To be Kenyan according to this writer means the use and support of Swahili.

The whole question about the relationship between identity and Swahili use in Kenya becomes important, even crucial, because Kenya is an artificially created nation. Its boundaries were created as a by-product of 19th century European political strategy (Oliver and Fage, 1962). The British, really interested in Egypt and the Suez Canal, and in contolling the source of the Nile, ultimately came to an agreement with Germany to demarcate separate "spheres of influence" in eastern Africa. The heterogeneous social unit of Kenya was the result of this decision. Kenya includes a number of distinct societies and prior to the unity supplied by the British colonial administration there was no indigenous political entity which could lay claim to significant territorial control.

At independence the only identity that mattered for the large majority of Kenyans beyond immediate family and kin group, was a localized ethnicity. There may have been an awareness of cultural and/or linguistic similarities and differences within large groupings, but there was no national or even regional identity. The British colonial administration may have served to broaden identity by delineating (and in some instances creating) "tribes" as administrative units which were of greater importance to the average Kenyan than membership in an entity called "Kenya" (Gulliver, 1969).

Certainly the efforts by missionary groups to codify vernaculars for the purpose of preparing biblical and religious materials helped in the formation of "tribal" units by supplying their linguistic symbols. In any event, "tribalism" is a worry of national planners in contemporary Kenya. Nationalistically minded leaders try to avoid tribal references--a standard political statement is to denounce "tribal" sentiments at least insofar as they conflict with national sentiments, and any suggestion that a tribal vernacular should become a national language would be met with hostile reaction. Under these circumstances Swahili should make an ideal national language: it does not have the connotation as a tribal language; it can stand by itself as a language with primarily Kenyan identity.

Kenya is a new nation. It has been independent for a little more than twelve years, and, prior to this, existed as a British colony for about 70 years. Among the critical problems Kenya must solve are the development of organizational efficiency, education systems, and economic self-sufficiency. In a sense these are technical problems of nation-building (Fishman 1968b; Whiteley, 1969) and in this connection a common objection to Swahili is that it lacks the technical vocabulary necessary for westernized nation-building especially in comparison with the rich technical vocabulary available in English.

Whiteley (1969: 120ff), discussing the problems of language development in regard to the creation of specialized terminologies, presents an example where the development of semantic elaboration results in a "connotational" overload for the Swahili term uchumi. The primary meaning of the verbal root from which it derived (-chum-) is "pluck, gather (especially fruit)." This meaning can be seen in other derived forms such as uchumaji wa buni "the picking of coffee." A second meaning, which Whiteley states was "already well established by the early sixties," is "making a profit." A third meaning, resulting from the extension of the term into economics, was "economy" or "commerce." As of 1966 Whiteley determined that there were at least five areas of meaning for uchumi in addition to its older, primary meaning "to pluck, gather": the economy, the national income, the gross domestic production or productive capacity (i.e. making a profit), and resources or funds available for investment (pp. 122-124). Whiteley concludes that this kind of excess connotational load,

> illustrates the kind of situation which is liable to develop during a period of rapid linguistic and political change. The intricacies of modern economic problems cannot be simplified beyond a certain point, and the language needs to be equipped to handle the necessary range of concepts in an unambiguous manner. (1969:125)

Whiteley's example of the range of meanings for uchumi could quite easily be viewed as a possible source for humor in a mode such as a joke--for example, one character says he is looking for uchumi [meaning "investment funds"] and another character directs him to a coffee plantation! A single joke is possible on any particular aspect of society, including any of the many ambiguities in natural human languages. The question to be answered in this study is whether there are some areas of repeated concern over language use in the jokes. There are (as Whiteley's example implies) many joke topic possibilities in the rapid development of Swahili. In fact, the problem of multiple connotations of a single term is only one source of possible confusion. Swahili-speakers use a large and increasing number of English loans, e.g. kilabu, "[night] club;" poketi mani, "pocket money;" baisikeli, "bicycle," Some of these are well established in the lexicon but many others are recent and consequently unfamiliar and confusing. Also Swahili-speakers are typically second language speakers and their speech usually exhibits varying degrees of interference with their first language both in choice of words and variations in form.

These conditions are symptoms of the stresses which modernization, Westernization (particularly the presence of English) and a second language status have placed upon Swahili. The question which will be examined in this study is whether speech misunderstandings which are based upon these possible communicational problems constitute areas of repeated concern in the content of Cheka na Baraza jokes.

CHAPTER I: MULTILINGUALISM IN KENYA

Kenya possesses a complex linguistic situation both because it encloses speakers of many different languages and because of the functional overlap among many of these languages. Although Kenya generally can be described as having a "three-language structure" (Nida and Wonderly 1971), it is not in a condition of functional equilibrium or diglossia. The uses of the two major lingua francas, Swahili and English, and the many vernaculars have never been clearly demarcated in any study except in the most general terms (e.g. Nida and Wonderly 1971; Whiteley 1969) and are undoubtedly changing in relation to one another. This must be especially so in regard to Swahili as its use expands through its development as an official language and, more recently, as a created national language.[1]

Vernacular Diversity

There are over 40 different languages in Kenya, most of them members of the Bantu, Nilotic, or Cushitic language groupings.[2] Speakers of Bantu languages comprise close to 65 percent of Kenya's population. In terms of numbers the most important members of the Bantu group are Kikuyu, Kamba, Luhya, Meru, Gusii, Embu, and Mijikenda. The next largest number of speakers (30 percent) is in the Nilotic group, and the numerically important members are Luo, Kalenjin, Turkana, and Masai. Three percent of the Kenyan population speak a Cushitic language, with only Somali being numerically important.

---

[1] Since the time of the research upon which this study is based (1972-73) Swahili has been officially designated as the national language of Kenya. Now, for example, it can be used (alongside English) in parliamentary debates.

[2] This classification is taken from that of Joseph Greenberg (1966). In his larger scheme, Greenberg places Bantu within the Benue-Niger substock of the Niger-Congo linguistic stock of languages; he places Nilotic within the Chari-Nile substock of the Nilo-Saharan linguistic stock, he places Cushitic as a substock of the Afroasiatic linguistic stock.

The rest of the languages spoken in Kenya cannot be grouped together structurally. They can be grouped historically as "foreign languages" in comparison with what might be called "indigenous languages." The most important of these are English, Gujerati, and Punjabi. Nairobi and Mombasa are international cities with small but diverse groups of immigrants and visitors, so a complete list of foreign languages is longer, but these languages are not at present a significant aspect of Kenya's language situation.

The speakers of only 13 languages (taking the languages spoken by Kenyan Asians as one "group") comprise over 93 percent of Kenya's total population. The number and distribution of these major languages are shown in Table 1.

Language Dialect and Language Variety Diversity

The list of language names given in Table 1 is actually a simplification. Kalenjin, for example, does not represent a single linguistic form but rather stands for a number of related forms, which include formerly "distinct" languages such as Nandi and Kipsigis. Based upon the recognition of their linguistic and social similarities, and the political advantages in unification, the speakers of Nandi and Kipsigis (and others) agreed to a standard written form called Kalenjin. Nandi and Kipsigis could now be called spoken dialects of standard Kalinjin, but without official written forms of their own. Similarly, the terms Luhya, Mijikenda, and Somali include many distinct dialects. The difference between "languages," in Kenya and elsewhere, is often as much a question of political and social identity as it is of linguistic distinctiveness (Haugen 1966).

The existence of recognizable dialects of single languages, however, is only one dimension of a complex language situation. Dialects are localized language varieties which are spoken as a first (or "mother tongue") language by a particular community. In addition to dialects, there may be other versions of a language that are spoken in a number of special situations for certain

TABLE 1: Number and location of the speakers of Kenyan vernaculars.

Vernacular	Number of Speakers as a First Language[a]	Percent of Total Population (10,942,705)[a]	Traditional Location
Kikuyu (B)[b]	2,201,632	20.2	Central highlands, southwest of Mt. Kenya (Central Province)
Luo (N)	1,521,595	13.9	Western savanna around Kavirondo Gulf on Lake Victoria (Nyanza Provinde)
Luhya (b)	1,453,302	13.3	Western savanna south of Mt. Elgon (Western Province)
Kamba (B)	1,197,712	11.0	East Central Plains (Eastern Province)
Kalenjin (N)	1,190,213	10.9	Discontinuous area in west around the middle portion of the Rift Valley and adjacent plateau (Rift Valley Province
Gusii (B)	701,679	6.5	Western savanna plateau southeast of Kavirondo Gulf (Nyanza Province)
Meru (B)	554,256	5.1	Central highlands on eastern slopes of Mt. Kenya (Eastern Province)
Mijikenda (B)	520,520	4.8	Coastal littoral and adjacent plains (Coastal Province)
Somali (C)	252,574	2.3	Northeastern arid plains (Northeastern Province)
Turkana (N)	203,177	1.9	Northwestern arid plains (Rift Valley Province)
Masai (N)	154,906	1.4	Southern grasslands (Rift Valley Province)
Asian group[c]	139,037	1.3	Scattered mainly in urban areas throughout country
Embu (B)	117,969	1.1	Central highlands on southeast slopes of Mt. Kenya (Eastern Province)
	Total Percent	93.7	

[a]Figures taken from Kenya Population Census, 1969, Vol. I:69.

[b]Letters in parenthesis indicate language grouping: B-Bantu, N-Nilotic, and C-Cushitic.

[c]The two major Asian languages are Gujerati and Punjabi.

If they are distinct forms, they can be called by a number of terms (e.g. "standard language," "jargon," "sociolect"), but I will simply use the neutral term "variety." The language names given above in Table 1 include not only different dialects, but also different varieties. All this heterogeneity can be illustrated with reference to Swahili.

Swahili Dialects and Varieties

There are many dialects of Swahili. They are dispersed all over East Africa: Chimiini, spoken at Brava on the Somali coast; Kinzwani spoken in the Comoro Islands, Kiunguja, spoken in Zanzibar City and, in closely related forms, farther south along the Tanzanian coast; Kimvita spoken in Mombasa; Kiamu spoken in Lamu; Chifundi spoken on the coast south of Mombasa, as well as several other dialects spread along the coast (Polomé 1967; Whiteley 1969).

Each Swahili-speaking community has several varieties of the language. Lienhardt in his general description of Swahili-speaking coastal communities comments on one variety:

> Far from being a crude sort of pidgin language, as some Europeans who know of it only in its up-country versions suppose, Swahili is remarkably rich and subtle . . . Both in literature and in daily speech there is a Kiswahili cha ndani, or 'internal Swahili', consisting of the inner meaning of words and phrases. These parts of verbal play serve the purposes of irony. (1968:2-3)

There is a rich literary tradition within the Swahili-speaking area of the East African coast, consequently there are literary varieties of Swahili (Harries 1962). Some of those which have received the greatest amount of attention are specifically written forms. If these are spoken at all, they are used only in performances such as the recitation of poetry. Some of these varieties are written in Arabic script (for example that based upon the Lamu dialect) and have been greatly influenced by Arabic literary, especially poetic, traditions. Some are written in Roman script. Only one of these latter varieties has any importance today in Kenya (and East Africa)--Standard Swahili. It was originally created by missionary-linguists on the model of the dialect spoken in Zanzibar City (Kiunguja); it received an official codification in 1930 (Whiteley 1969) and is an official written form for all government, technical, business and educational affairs in Kenya and Tanzania. The term "Swahili" therefore represents a range of linguistic dialects and functional varieties, including the official written form of Standard Swahili.

Second Language Diversity

Kenya is a nation composed of multilingual individuals who often use more than one language; varieties of English, Arabic, other vernaculars, and, especially, Swahili are used throughout Kenya as second languages. Indeed, the importance of Swahili and English in Kenya is not due to their use as vernaculars; they do not appear on Table 1 because the number of first language speakers of both is less than one percent of Kenya's population. According to the 1969 Kenya Population Census, Swahili is listed as the first language of only 35,000 Kenyans (0.3 percent of the total population) and English as the first language of about 40,000 (0.4 percent).[1]

There are many spoken varieties of Swahili which are used as second languages. With few exceptions these do not have names and have not recived any scientific study. They are distinctive because each exhibits varying degrees of marked interference with one of Kenya's vernaculars.[2]

---

[1] The figures for English speakers is an overestimate because the population census only lists "Europeans" and some of these speak other European languages as a first language.

[2] There are no descriptions of the exact manner in which Swahili is learned as a second language. Some part of this process occurs in formal educational settings and involves only Standard Swahili as a model. Harries, in fact, makes the claim that "Mainland Africans learn their Swahili at school from standard forms". (1968: 428). But Gorman states that his data, ". . . bear out the general assumption that a knowledge of Swahili is characteristically acquired outside the formal educational system" (1971:205). Learned in less formal situations, such as in conversations with neighbors or with shopkeepers, Swahili forms would undoubtedly exhibit at least some interference with a vernacular.

One of these interference-marked varieties (IMV) which does have a name and has been (partially) described is Kisettla. It is characteristically spoken between the (British) European settlers and their African servants, and exhibits a great amount of lexical and grammatical interference from English. An example of Kisettla is the sentence Tia scones ndani oven and lete chai pot ("Put the scones in the oven and bring the tea pot") which is a mixture of English word order and English and Swahili lexemes (J.W., no date but approximately 1930). (The published accounts of Kisettla do not mention phonological interference although there is no doubt that it occurs.) Another IMV, somewhat similar in use to Kisettla, is Kihindi, which refers to the forms used between Asians and their African servants and exhibits interference from an Asian language such as Gujerati or Punjabi (Neale 1972). In addition there are the IMV's of Swahili marked by interference with the vernaculars.

Diversity in the Use of Swahili and English as Second Languages

The diversity of second language use has many dimensions. The frequency with which a second language is used, the various communicative functions for which it is used, and the relative proficiency of its use are all important considerations. Where there is more than one second language, as in Kenya, a complicating factor is that the same speaker may speak several languages. Most Kenyans use Swahili and many also use English. Yet given the changes that have occurred in Swahili's position within the last decades, a Kenyan who uses both Swahili and English may not use them in completely separate situations. When Nida and Wonderly (1971) use Kenya as an example of a nation having a three language structure--characterized by the complementary functional allocation of the vernaculars, Swahili and English--they are speaking at a very general level. Whereas this characterization is not wholly incorrect, there are Kenyan families for whom Swahili (although not as their vernacular) is the language used at home; some Kenyans who use English to converse with Kenyans of different ethnic backgrounds, and, increasingly, Kenyans who use Swahili to transmit technical matters within the country. This is not to imply that second language use in Kenya has no pattern, but rather that the allocation of second language is changing and an individual may often not be sure which second language is appropriate in a particular situation. If there were only monolingualism in Kenya--if each speaker used just his first language--then the distribution of language functions would equal the distribution of language speakers. Furthermore, there would be no differentiation among these languages in terms of their functions each would be used in equivalent social situations and for all communicative purposes.

This hypothetical situation is not too far from the actual language situation in Kenya. In terms of frequency of use the thirteen languages in Table 1 undoubtedly account for most of the speech forms used in most of the language functions in social interaction. Child socialization, family discussions, social sanctions, gossip, cooperative work projects, community social organizations--most of these are performed in one of these first languages. But in one important respect this hypothetical situation does not accurately represent Kenya's language situation; neither Swahili nor English is used by any large group of speakers as a first language, yet each has great functional importance due to its use as a second language. For certain communicative functions one or the other, or both, of these two languages has the highest, in some cases the only frequencies of occurrence.

It is not possible to construct a tabular presentation of the number of speakers, readers and writers of Swahili and English as second languages as was done for the first languages because not enough information is available. Tabulating first language uses can be relatively easy since obviously a large number of functions can be summed up by simply stating that a first language is used for <u>all</u> the communicative and social requirements of the groups of first language speakers. In order to delineate second language use and function it is necessary to describe the distinctive features of the social, symbolic, and physical context of just those situations in which the language occurs. Detailed information is lacking, but based upon the accumulated research on language use in Kenya, particularly the works of Whiteley, Gorman, and Parkin, it is possible to estimate the probable second language uses of Swahili and English.

In education there is a fairly clear use difference among Kenya's languages according to educational level. All college and secondary school, and most of the later primary instruction is in English. Most early primary instruction is in English. Most early primary instruction is in one of the first language vernaculars. In the middle primary standards there is a change-over so that by the last primary standards instruction is in English. Swahili's use in education is in flux. Prior to World War II, it had a much greater functional role as a medium of instruction but has since been largely replaced by English (Gorman 1971b). Typically, in most schools now Swahili is taught as a subject but is not used as a medium of instruction.

The most desirable ordering of languages, from the point of view of many education officials, is to introduce English as early as possible in primary education so as to have more English experience prior to secondary school. The language used in the beginning primary standards would then be any language that would best serve as the introductory medium to formal education. This might be a vernacular for a primary school (usually rural) which consisted entirely of the speakers of the vernacular, but it might be Swahili for a primary school (usually urban) which consisted of speakers of different vernaculars.

In the communications media--radio, television, motion pictures, and newspapers--English and Swahili are the major mediums of expression. The national radio broadcasts consist of the National Service in Swahili and the General Service in English each having roughly the same airtime. Nevertheless, the broadcasts are not identical. Popular music and news are given in both (a classical music program is on the English service, however), as is the East African Safari commentary, but soccer matches are on the Swahili service whereas overseas rugby scores are on the English service. The commentary immediately following a speech by President Kenyatta is in Swahili. Generally, a radio listener has access to fairly equal frequencies of Swahili and English broadcasts, except during the mid-day broadcasting period when school broadcasts are aired primarily in English. There are regional services which broadcast

TABLE 2
Circulation figures for Kenyan newspapers

Title	Language	Circulation[a]
Daily		
East African Standard	English	36,000
Daily Nation	English	20,000
Taifa Leo	Swahili	17,000
Weekly		
East African Standard Friday Edition	English	49,000
Baraza	Swahili	40,000
Sunday Nation	English	32,000
Taifa Kenya	Swahili	31,000
Sauti ya Mwafrika	Swahili	19,000
Sunday Post	English	16,000
Africa Samachar	Gujerati	16,000
Kiri-Nyaga	Kikuyu	15,000

[a]Figures are taken from the Area Handbook for Kenya, pp. 386-390, and are based upon the newspapers' self-reported circulation for 1963. It should be noted that some of these figures represent an East African circulation, not just Kenyan. The figure given for Baraza, for example, probably represents its total circulation for Kenya, Tanzania, and Uganda--and the same is undoubtedly true for most of the other newspapers in the Table.

in a number of vernaculars, as well as the Asian group.

Television broadcasts are weighted more toward English. The daily opening program (5:00 p.m.) is news and commentary in Swahili. There are some Swahili situation comedies, theatre productions, and public service programs, but a large number of programs are imported from America and Britain and are in English. In this medium, unlike radio, only the two official languages are used--no vernaculars are broadcast. Television broadcasts at this writing are limited to the Nairobi and Mombasa areas.

The movie Mlevi (the Drunkard) released several years ago is still the only full length Swahili film made in Kenya. There are Swahili documentaries produced for instructional and developmental programs, but screen entertainment in primarily in English or in one of the languages of the Asian group. Those few foreign language films which are shown (a film in Arabic on the life of Mohammed, Chinese karate epics) have sub-titles in English.

Of the three daily newspapers with a circulation greater than 10,000, two are in English and one is in Swahili, and of eight major weeklies, three are in English, three are in Swahili, one is in Gujerati and the other is in Kikuyu. Just adding the circulation of these newspapers, in one week's period 153,000 copies of English newspapers are published versus 107,600 copies of Swahili newspapers.

In government communications, both Swahili and English are official languages. President Kenyatta's national speeches are delivered first in English and then in Swahili. Debates in Parliament and all higher court proceedings are in English, but most of the public petitions to district and location officers are in Swahili. For much of the rest, both languages are used. It is possible to obtain a passport, register a birth, get a driver's license, or apply for a business license in either English or Swahili. It is difficult to estimate the relative frequencies of each language although when all government business is taken together Swahili probably predominates. (An unknown factor is the use of local languages; they are not sanctioned for governmental use, but they probably are, in fact, used.)

In business and technical activities, both Swahili and English are used. In transactions of international or national scope, English is used more frequently than Swahili, due, in no small part, to the economic ties that Kenya has with Britain and English-speaking countries.[1]

But in the everyday small scale business arrangements conducted between speakers of different first languages, Swahili must have a much greater frequency than English. Most investigators readily agree that Swahili's strength, and its most important second language function, lies in its use as a lingua franca of ordinary business transactions (from ordering a drink to cashing a check) in the cities, towns, and rural centers where speaker members of different languages meet.

---

[1]For example, during this research while attempting to have a questionnaire typed in Swahili at a secretarial school, I was told by the school principal that there was a greater demand for secretaries skilled in English rather than Swahili.

CHAPTER II: SWAHILI AS AN OBJECT OF BELIEF IN KENYA

> A Kenyan who claims to know English or any other language and professes ignorance of Kiswahili should be despised and known as "koroboi" . . .[1] (Robert Matano, quoted in the Sunday Nation, April 5, 1970)

> Generally speaking they [advanced level students] see Swahili as a language that cannot help them in their future career advancement. (Welime 1970)

These two statements were published in the same year. Although different in purpose, they express the opposing points of view that characterize Swahili today: Swahili as a necessary second language and Swahili as an unnecessary second language. In a nation of diverse languages and ethnic groupings, Swahili could provide the essential function of serving as a common means of communication and a common symbol of national identity for all Kenyans. But national communication and identity can be affected by the beliefs which Kenyans have about Swahili. The language is used in many situations of inter-ethnic contact, and as a medium of most kinds of national communication; should Kenya's leaders consequently assume that Kenyans believe Swahili is a neutral, non-tribal language?

The statement made by Robert Matano, then Acting Secretary-General of KANU, is an emotional appeal about what Kenyans should (or rather, should not) be doing in regard to language choice. This statement represents a recent stage in an historical progression, begun over a century ago, which has seen Swahili change its position from a vernacular spoken primarily in the trading cities along the East African coast (and probably then believed to be inferior to Arabic) to a widely used second language believed to be particularly useful in the cause of nationalism and national communication. The value of Swahili has several dimensions. For some, Swahili is seen as an African language in specific contrast to English. Of course,

---

[1] Koroboi is a personal term of derogation, generally carrying the meaning of a European lackey.

others may view Swahili, with its large number of lexical loans from Arabic, as being a foreign language or, worse, given its early association with slavery, as the lingua franca of the slave caravans, as a language of African exploitation. For some Kenyans Swahili's suitability is due to its affinity with other Bantu languages, which makes it easier for speakers of other Bantu languages to learn, and also gives it a "Bantu," as well as a national, identity. However, almost 32 percent of Kenya's population does not share the specific "Bantu" identity and would not believe that Swahili was an easy language to learn. Some Kenyans believe that Swahili is suitable as a national language simply becuase it has no specific ethnic identity. Wilfred Whiteley (once an active participant in the development of Standard Swahili as Chairman of the Interterritorial Language [Swahili] Committee) states this belief concisely," . . . what was loved by none could be tolerated by all!" (Whiteley 1969:12). This may be the best reason for the use of Swahili as a medium of national communication. Yet Matano's appeal for derogation of Kenyans who may not know Swahili would indicate that a "national" symbol must be the object of more than the absence of any strong emotion.

The Welime quotation at the beginning of this chapter was made by an educator concerned by the problems of advanced-level Swahili instruction. The statement is an unemotional assessment of secondary students' views about the desirability of advanced study in Swahili; it represents a current stage in a seesaw weighting of the relative advantages of Swahili and English.

The early European officials in East Africa were engaged in several activities that involved the formation of language policies affecting the use of Swahili. Missionaries required a language of proselytization and a language of Christian education and government officials required a language of native affairs. Faced with the fact of the linguistic diversity among inland peoples, Europeans generally agreed upon Swahili, already known as a lingua franca in the interior. It seemed an efficient and economical solution to the need for a common means of widespread communication among the peoples of the colonial territory. Europeans would only need to learn, where necessary, a single language. The business of governing--preparing directives to local leaders, arranging for the recruitment of labor, etc.--could all be conducted in Swahili. A junior civil service of African clerks could all be trained in one language.

Had all the Europeans maintained this consistent policy towards the development of Swahili in Kenya, its functional importance as an official language would undoubtedly be greater today. However, while the Europeans increased the use of Swahili by encouraging it as a lingua franca for ordinary affairs and the marketplace, at the same time they weakened its functional importance by encouraging the use of English as the language of higher education and national affairs and maintaining the use of pidgin variety of Swahili such as Kisletta as a medium of European-African communication.

In education, Swahili's position was equivocal in relation to the vernaculars and English. Missionaries, who developed and staffed most schools until World War II, were often of the opinion that the local language was all that was needed as a medium of instruction. A local language would be a more effective means of imparting Christian learning than a "foreign" language like Swahili which was often considered to be a "Muslim" language. It was felt also that the training of a Christian, Westernized elite who ultimately would be the leaders of African societies in East Africa should be in English and not in Swahili.

Despite the European encouragement of the vernaculars and English, many Africans still considered Swahili a useful second language. The opportunities open to those who only spoke a local language were limited and there were few, if any, openings for English-speaking Africans until late in the colonial period. The junior civil service, as well as jobs as messengers, clerks and servants, depended upon the ability to use some Swahili, and African education and opportunity depended upon Swahili as the basic medium for much of the colonial period. Linguists, writers, educators and other authorities interested in the development of Swahili have performed considerable labors on the codification and description of

Standard Swahili's grammer, phonology (including the orthography of its Roman script), and vocabulary. But the resources for post-primary education were never really developed for Swahili, and higher education, when offered, was given in English. At the same time, after World War II and continuing past independence, more and more English-using opportunities were open to Africans.

Given the resources available in English as a world language, and the fact that similar resources were not developed for Swahili, there was no contest. Swahili could not compete with English as a second language in those national economic, technical, and governmental affairs which had been developed and were still controlled by English speakers, and which required an educational background only available in English. Thus there is Welime's statement that in 1970 students saw no advantage in Swahili.

Can it be inferred that these students also believed that Swahili was incapable of efficiently communicating the national, technical topics which have been dominated by the use of English?

There can be little doubt that language use in general and the use of Swahili in particular are of some concern to Kenyans. This is to be expected given the diverse, and changing, language situation. These questions regarding beliefs about Swahili--its neutrality and its communicational efficiency and effectiveness--are important both to a fuller understanding of Swahili's position in contemporary Kenya, and to the decisions which Kenya's social planners must make concerning the formation of language planning programs. The large number of linguistic descriptions of the structure of Swahili, as valuable as they are for the processes of codification and standardization, are not sufficient to answer these questions. The future development of Swahili will be influenced by the beliefs and attitudes which Kenyans themselves have about its use.

CHAPTER III: THE CHEKA NA BARAZA JOKES

Baraza: A General Service Newspaper

Baraza is a Swahili-language newspaper published each Thursday in Nairobi for distribution throughout Kenya, and East Africa.[1] It is a subsidiary of the East African Standard (Newspapers) Ltd., which also publishes the English-language East African Standard. Baraza is aimed at a general Kenyan and East African readership and offers a variety of local, national, and international news and feature material. It is one of the five largest newspapers in Kenya and has the largest circulation of any Swahili-language newspaper. Baraza is a commercial operation and is therefore actively oriented toward increasing its circulation and advertising revenues. Over the last several years, it has been markedly successful, at least insofar as circulation figures indicate. Based upon information supplied by Baraza's advertising department, its circulation had increased from a little under 43,000 in 1971 to over 60,000 at the beginning of 1973. In part, Baraza's popularity is due to the efforts by its long-time editor, Francis Khamisi, to popularize its content. A large proportion of each issue is devoted to future columns on a variety of popular topics.

Baraza is not, it should be noted, a Swahili copy of the East African Standard. For some of its news, Baraza is dependent upon the facilities of the Standard but Baraza is otherwise independent of the Standard and has its own editorial policies and control over what it prints.

The typical Baraza issue has eight pages. Occasionally, a special supplement will be included as an extra section in the

---

[1]In 1969, Baraza was distributed among Kenya, Tanzania, and Uganda in the following proportions: Kenya 61 percent, Tanzania 32 percent, and Uganda 7 percent.

center of the newspaper. It is a full-sized paper--not a tabloid. Each page has an area of newsprint measuring 16 by 22 inches which is organized into eight two-inch vertical columns. Technically, Baraza is a good quality newspaper due to the efforts of its experienced staff and to its production by the printing facilities of the East African Standard. There are many photographs throughout the paper, and the advertisements are often in color. The newsprint is clear and there seems to be few serious typographical errors.

Baraza is usually described as being produced for a general African readership (Kitchen 1956; Ainslie 1966; Feuereisen and Schmacke 1969). In fact, Baraza is not designed exclusively for Africans since much of its content--world and national news, the astrology columns, and the editor's page--would be of interest to a Kenyan or an East African reader of any origin. But Baraza is written in Swahili,[1] and this effectively limits the readership primarily to Africans, who are most of the literate users of Swahili in Kenya.

Baraza is also aimed at a "national" readership in the very important sense that it is not a "tribal" publication. Its two highest editorial positions, for example, are not filled by members of any of the large ethnic groups but by coastal Kenyans. Furthermore, Baraza gives no special preference to ethnic news; local affairs included usually are events of national or regional significance. For example, a meeting of the Mombasa branch of the Kamba Union is reported, but mostly in regard to their statement of support for the spirit of national independence.

---

[1]Small sections are written in English, e.g. some advertisements or parts of advertisements, and some of the classified ads and announcements. These do not amount to any significant part of the newspaper, they merely are proof that English has been the dominant language of business and official publications.

An Overview of Baraza's Content

It is useful at this point to examine the contents of one issue of Baraza. The April 12, 1973 issue was chosen because this is the one preceding the Cheka na Baraza joke contest whose entries form the basis of this study. The first announcement of the contest appeared in the April 5th issue and the second in the April 12th issue. The April 12th edition while generally representative at least of the manner in which Baraza was produced in 1973, is specifically an example of its content at the start of the ten week period during which the data for this study was collected. It is in no way special or unusual. The space allocated to the various sections of the paper, and their positioning in the paper, differ from one issue to the next, of course. For example, in the April 19th issue the column on teenage music is smaller (11 percent of one page rather than 13 percent[1]) and Cheka na Baraza has been moved to page 3 from page 6 and has been enlarged (6.5 percent rather than 4 percent). But the April 12th issue is essentially representative of Baraza in 1973.

The non-advertising contents of the April 12th issue are as follows. The first page consists of national and international news, and a large column about fortune-telling (Dunia Wiki Hii). Page 2 is mostly taken up with the editor's column of vituko--reader-contributed tales of human foibles, usually of a sexual or marital nature--(Panapofuka Moshi Panaficha Moto) along with a small column about popular teenage music (Ulimwengu wa Musiki na Vijana). Page 3 contains a small question-and-answer column (Mwulize Mzee Upara) and a large column describing recent--and usually sensational--court cases (Macho Yetu Kortini).

---

[1]These and all the following percentages in this section refer to the proportion of an entry to a full page using column-inches as a measure, one full page equals 170 column-inches.

Page 4 is the editorial page accompanied by a large section of letters to the editor. Page 5 has more national news and world news, a reader-contributed short story, and a small column with a religious message (Fikara Kwa Juma Hili). Page 6 has sport news and game scores, and includes small sections of the Cheka na Baraza column, pen pal requests (Urafiki wa Kalamu), and a crossword puzzle contest. Page 7 contains a large section with readers' greetings (Salamu), a small column of marriage requests (Kutafuta Mchumba) and a large column of reader-contributed poetry (Mashairi Yenu Matamu). The last page contains local and national news, several announcements and the week's horoscope (Nyota Zenu).

News and sports together occupy about 32 percent of Baraza's non-advertising space.[1] Feature columns written by staff members (eg. an astrology column, editorial, teenage music) or invited authors (a religious message) make up 13 percent of the total newspaper's non-advertising space. The other half is taken up with reader-contributed material--eg. the editor's column of vituko, readers' greetings, poetry and fiction and Cheka na Baraza.

---

[1]Advertising occupied a little over 30 percent of the total newspaper space. As might be expected, most of these ads are for Western (i.e. non-traditional) manufactured products--beauty soap, toothpaste, phonograph records, laundry detergent. Further, none of these products are really expensive. This is undoubtedly more of a refelection of the opinion advertisers have of Baraza's readership than of the buying practices of the readers themselves. One advertising executive told me informally that, although they had no data on Swahili-language newspaper readership, he assumed that they would not be as affluent as an English-language readership.

The Orientation of Readers' Letters to the Editor

Baraza is clearly a readers' newspaper. Half of its non-advertising content is directly or indirectly (i.e., partly re-written) a product of readers who write to the newspaper and thereby communicate their greetings, opinions and jokes to other readers. These expressions are a standard, on-going aspect of the newspaper and undoubtedly contribute to its popularity.

An important aspect of these readers' comments is that their subject matter is not esoteric or personal, but is much more likely to be about matters of general interest--national affairs, contemporary behavior of youth, education, sex and marriage. The most personal of the reader-contributed columns, "Warm Greetings," is so standardized that, while the names differ, the messages are alike. The other personal columns--"Penpals" and "Looking for a Spouse"--do provide some information about the writers, such as sex, age, and education. The rest of the reader-contributed columns, however, provide information about the way in which the writer views or is concerned about matters whose scale is larger than the writer's personal situation. In the poetry column, Letters to the Editor, and the editor's column of vituko, subjects are discussed which should be widely understood by most, if not all, of Baraza's readers. Conversely, these columns should yield information about the writers' beliefs and attitudes toward general topics and aspects of Kenyan and East African life, including the use of Swahili as a symbol and a medium of nation-building and in relation to other languages.

This is an important assumption. It bears directly upon the manner in which I am using the content of the Cheka na Baraza jokes as a source of information regarding beliefs about language use. Consequently, to strengthen the assumption that readers' expressions are mostly about topics of a general interest, I sought a further demonstration in the Letters to the Editor column for a one year period--from November 2, 1972 to November 1, 1973. This period bracketed the ten weeks in April-June 1973 during which the jokes for this study were collected. Of all the letters sampled,

31 percent were references to personal, or local, matters: 13 percent referred to matters of at least regional concern, and 56 percent were about national, African, or world affairs.

The sample consisted of 52 letters randomly selected from each of the 52 issues of Baraza within the one year period. Each letter in an issued was assigned a two digit number--the first digit the column number counting from the left of the page, and the second the order in which the letter was placed in the column from the top. For example, the third letter down in the sixth column would be identified as "63." Using a table of random numbers one letter was taken from each issue.[1]

The letters were then examined as to the generality of their topical reference. Each letter was assigned to one of five categories reflecting scope of reader interest and concern: Personal--the writer and a limited group of other readers; local--readers familiar with a single, small locale (a township, location, or neighborhood); regional--readers familiar with a single, large locale (city, district, or province); national--readers familiar with Kenyan, Tanzanian or Ugandan affairs which are performed by the government or other nation-wide institution, or which are not limited to any particular part of the country but which could take place and be of interest anywhere; and East African, African and world. Some examples of letters placed in each of these categories are given below:[2]

> personal--condolences to relatives and friends of the recently deceased. . . (6-28-73 issue)
>
> local--more toilets should be built at Mudete [market center in Western Province] market (5-16-73 issue)

---

[1]Many letters occupied more than one column. Regardless of where a letter began, it was assigned a column order number for all of the columns in which it appeared. For example, a letter which began as the first letter in column seven but which continued as the first entry in column eight could be selected both as "71" and as "81." The sample was therefore skewed toward larger letters which would have more likelihood of occurring in more than one column.

[2]These examples have been taken only from Kenyan Letters to the Editor.

police station needed at Maseno [rural center in Nyansa Province] (2-15-73 issue)

regional--Complaint about trash collection in Mombasa (5-3-73 issue)

Behavior of some youths are giving a bad reputation to Luhya [tribe] and Western Province (4-5-73 issue)

national--"Strong men" [men who tour the country exhibiting feats of their strength] should compete for Kenya in the Olympics (12-14-72 issue)

Smoking should be prohibited in buses (11-16-72 issue)

Increase in building fund contributions from Sh. 10/- to 100/- makes school fees too high (3-1-73 issue)

Praise of Kenya's progress under leadership of President Kenyatta (7-12-73 issue)

East African, African, and World --Problems of African continent due to the quarrels of its leaders (4-12-73 issue)

Disapproval of church marriage of two men in the United States (11-23-72)

The distribution of letters in these categories is shown in Table 2.

TABLE 3. Distribution of letters to the editor by topic and country of origin

	TOPIC (GENERALITY OF REFERENCE)					
COUNTRY	East African, African, and World	National	Areal	Local	Personal	Total
Kenya (% of row)	2 (8%)	11 (42%)	5 (19%)	6 (23%)	2 (8%)	26
Tanzania and Uganda (% Of row)	3 (12%)	13 (50%)	2 (8%)	4 (15%)	4 (15%)	26
Total (% of total)	5 (10%)	24 (46%)	7 (13%)	10 (19%)	6 (12%)	52

Letters referring to matters of interest at regional or wider scale constitute almost 70 percent of the sample. It should be noted as well that most of the letters, regardless of the generality of their topic, refer to modern, Western-influenced conditions; toilets, school fees, police stations, trash collections, smoking on buses. We can assume that the other Baraza reader-contributed materials--specifically Cheka na Baraza jokes--will also be oriented toward general, modern experiences.[1]

Form and Content of Cheka na Baraza Jokes

Even a cursory glance at the contents of the April 12 issue of Baraza shows that it is as much a form of entertainment as it is newspaper. Its joke column, Cheka na Baraza, was begun as an attempt to add to entertainment appeal.[2]

On May 9, 1968, the following announcement appeared in Baraza:

> Jokes!
> We know that our readers really get a lot of enjoyment from our columns Where There's Smoke There's Fire and Our Eyes in Court.
> But Baraza is still looking for ways of pleasing our readers.
> Therefore starting next week we will bring you a new column of jokes.
> We want to join with our readers in pleasing them. Therefore readers

---

[1]Although the particular topic of language use did not appear in this sample of letters, it did appear within the total year's letters. There were 18 letters concerning language, 11 of these were from Kenyan writers. (For the year as a whole 1,112 letters were printed and these 18 letters represent only 1.6 percent of this total.) The content of these letters, with one exception concerning Swahili slang words is Nakuru (a city in the Rift Valley Province), would have been all categorized as "national."

[2]I was told by the editor, Francis Khamisi, that the Cheka na Baraza column was one of his ideas aimed specifically at generating greater reader interest in Baraza.

> are able to send jokes to be printed in this column. Nor should you worry because we are ready to pay (for the jokes).[1]

With the issue after this request for reader-contributed jokes (vichekesho),[2] the column Cheka na Baraza was started. It has appeared, containing about 5 jokes, in almost every issue since the Over one thousand jokes have been published and many times this number have been received by the newspaper.

The column is usually located on an inside page. Unlike some other columns, such as the editor's column Panapofuka Moshi Panaficha Moto which is always on page two, Cheka na Baraza is moved around as space considerations dictate. It is one of the last columns to be composed, and so must be fitted into whatever space is left, but it is easily recognized by its distinctive

---

[1] Vichekesho!
Sisi twajua sana kwamba wasomaji wetu wengi hucheka mpaka wakavunjika mbavu kwa makala zetu za Panapofuka Moshi Panaficha Moto na pia Macho Yetu Kortini.

Lakini Baraza bado inatafuta njia za kufurahisha na kuchangamsha wasomaji wake.

Kwa hivyo toka wiki hii ijayo tutawaletea makala mpya ya vichekesho.

Hapa pia tunataka kuungana na wasomaji wetu katika kazi za kuwafurahisha na kuwatumika. Kwa hivyo wasomaji wetu wanaweza kutuletea vichekesho ambavyo tutavichapa katika makala hayo. Wala wasiwe na wasiwasi, kwani kiinua mgongo tayari tutatoa kuwapa.

[2] Vichekesho (singular-Kichekesho) will be used here to refer to those written newspaper "jokes." The term translates quite easily into English as "jokes" since it is a derivation of the verb stem chekesha, "to cause to laugh". For the rest of this study I will simply use the English term "joke" and "jokes" instead of Kichekesho and Vichekesho, but I wish to make it clear that by using these English terms I do not intend to include all other meanings of "joke" in English.

banner which has the legend "*Cheka na Baraza*" over the drawing of the faces of many people who are apparently laughing quite strongly (see Figure 1).

FIGURE 1: Reproduction of the *Cheka na Baraza* column banner.

Characteristics of the Jokes: The Lead and the Exchange

The jokes all share a similar form. Each joke is a depiction of what, in sociolinguistic terms, would be called a series of "speech acts" (Hymes 1962; Fishman 1972b). As an illustration, we can examine a joke which appeared in one of the first columns (June 13, 1968):

> Mzee mmoja mwenye madeni chungu mzima alimwona mdai wake akienda kwake kudai haki yake. Aliingia nyumbani na kumwambia mtoto wake kama mtu huyo akifika amwambie amekwenda safari:
>
> Mdai wake: Mtoto, baba yake yuko wapi?
> Mtoto: Ameisha kwenda safari ndefu.
> Mdai wake: Atarudi Lini?
> Mtoto: Ngoja hapo nje niende uikamwulize!!

The beginning paragraph (lines 1-5) serves as an introduction to the verbal exchange between the characters. It may indicate the setting, the topic, and the social relationship of the characters including, perhaps, something about their motivations or emotional state. The above introduction can be translated as follows:

> [line 1] An old man [mzee] who has heavy debts [madeni] coming due [line 2] saw his creditor [mdai wake] coming to his home to collect [line 3] his debt. He goes "inside the house" [nyumbani] and tells [line 4] his young child [mtoto] [that] if that person [creditor] arrives the child is to tell him that [line 5] he [old man] has just gone on a long journey [safari]:

This introduction sets up the conversation which follows between the creditor and the old man's child. It supplies information abou several aspects of their speech interaction. The old man [mzee] is obviously not prepared or willing to pay for the debt which the creditor (mdai) is anxious to collect since he has come to the old man's house to get it. The old man devises a ruse using a young child (mtoto) who does not really understand the full significance of what his father wants him to do. The introduction supplies some information on the setting--the old man's home; the topics--the whereabouts of the old man; and the role relationship of the speakers--a stranger, who is a creditor, and a young child.

The rest of the joke contains the conversation between the characters. Each character is depicted as speaking in turn, each speech marked at the beginning by a character designation. This part can be translated as follows:

> Creditor: Child, where is your father?
> Child: He has just left on a long journey.
> Creditor: When will he return?
> Child: Wait here outside, I'll go ask him.

The child responds to the creditor's first question exactly as he was told by his father. But being without instruction for the creditor's second question he gives his father away. Aside from th particular content (and humor) of this joke, it represents the usu form for Cheka na Baraza. Depictions are of verbal interactions.

For the purposes of this study, I will use the terms "lead"

and "exchange" to refer to these two sections of the jokes. The lead is all of the introductory and supplementary descriptive commentary in the joke, and the exchange is just the depiction of the speech of the characters.

Not all jokes contain a lead. Often a joke consists only of an exchange, as the following example shows (taken from the July 4, 1968 column):

Askari katika zamu: Simama wewe au
utakamatwa na mbwa.
Mwizi: Ndiyo, najua kuwa mimi
siye mamako wala babako.

This joke can be translated as:

Guard on Watch: Stop [Simama] you or you
will be set upon by a dog [mbwa].
Thief: It is indeed so [Ndiyo], I know that
I am not your mother [mamako]
nor your father [babako].[1]

There is no lead in this joke. It begins with the first character's speech and contains no other descriptive statements. The joke consists only of an exchange.

Of course, the presence or absence of a lead is important only insofar as the analyses of the jokes are concerned where it is useful to be able to contrast the forms of language used in writing each part. A lead is not a necessary part of a joke--sufficient contextual information about the speech event in the exchange can be supplied as well by the character designations. In the example here the designations "guard on watch" (Askari katika zamu) and "thief" (Mwizi) tell something of the setting--probably around a building or house; the topic--a challenge, and the social

[1] The thief's answer here revolves around a play upon the guards initial command to halt "simama". -Simama is a verbal root meaning "to stand, to stand still, to stop." It is used here as an imperative form without any tense or person prefixes. The thief has rather chosen to interpret it as a combination of si (present negative of "to be") and mama "mother" and meaning something like "[you] are not [my] mother."

relationship of the speakers--one of a professional opposition.

In some jokes, leads, or parts of leads, are located within the exchange. In the following example (taken from the October, 1968 column) there is a beginning lead (lines 1-5) describing how Sheikh Ali has been unable to locate the post office and his meeting with the youth Juma. The exchange begins with Sheikh Ali asking Juma for directions and Juma's response. After Juma's response there is a commentary note (in parentheses, lines 9-10) telling how easily Juma directs Sheikh Ali. This commentary can be considered as a part of the joke's lead.

> Muhubiri mmoja ambaye alijulikana kama Sheikh Ali alipata taabu kubwa sana alipokuwa akitafuta njia ya kwenda posta na kuikosa kabisa. Akakutana na kijana mmjoa [sic] ambaye alijulikana kama Juma na mazungumzo yao yakaanza:
>
> Sheikh Ali: Kijana Juma, tangu asubuhi mpaka sasa ni saa nane natafuta njia ya kwenda posta siioni, tafadhali nisaidie mwanangu.
>
> Juma: Njoo nitakupeleka. (Juma akampeleka mzee mpaka posta kwa muda wa dakika tano tu). . . .

This joke can be translated as follows:

> [line 1] A preacher [muhubiri] known as Sheikh [lines 2-3] Ali became lost looking for the way [njia] to the post office. [lines 3-5] He met a youth [kijana] known as Juma and their conversation [mazmgumzo] began:
>
> Sheikh Ali: Youth Juma, since this morning it has been eight hours I am looking for the way to the post office, please help me my son [mwanangu].
>
> Juma: Come, I will take you. (Juma takes the old man to the post office in only five minutes.). . .[1]

The lead is all the parts of a joke which describe what the characters are doing but which are not themselves representations

---

[1] The conclusion of this joke which is omitted here for brevity, is that the preacher is so grateful that he invites Juma to come to his house and he will tell him the way to heaven. Juma tells him that if he cannot know the way to the post office how can he know the way to heaven.

of the character's speech.

The exchange of a joke is that part which is a direct representation of the character's speech. In each of the examples given above (to illustrate the lead) the exchange is clearly marked with each character depicted speaking in turn; his name or description is given and then his speech. Each character's speech has been represented by standard Swahili but that is not always the case. The importance of the exchange (and the importance of the jokes as documents on language use) is that it is often an attempt by the joke author to represent the actual speech of certain characters. Therefore, the speech representations in the exchange are not limited to standard forms. Instead, the exchange is often an attempt to depict speech as it is spoken, and heard, by the joke characters.

Arrangement of Joke Components

The identification of the lead and the exchange are not difficult for printed jokes and can even be done without a knowledge of Swahili due to the presence of certain formal distinguishing characteristics. Leads are printed in italics; exchanges are headed by the character designation in bold face type and the speech is separated from the character designation by a colon. This particular form is, to some extent, an artifact of the printing operation, and especially of secretarial editing.

The printed joke is a secondary document which is based upon the form of the joke actually written by the joke authors. In many instances there is no significant difference since joke authors have carefully written or typed their jokes in conformance with the way that the printed jokes appear in the newspaper--without the use of italics or bold-face type. Other jokes, as written by their authors, deviate from the printed form. These may be edited by the Baraza secretaries to conform to this printed arrangement when they are typeset. An example of this editing comparing an original joke copy with its typed copy is as follows:

Joke Original[1]

Mtoto [1]

Mama Kwanini ninyi
Wewe na Baba
Mnaonea watoto kama
Mimi wakikosa.

Mama [2]

Kwa kweli hatuwaonei
bali ni vitendo vyao
hufanya waonewe na
hata kupigwa.

Mtoto [3]

Mbona basi Ramadhani
si mtoto kama mimi
na mmesema mlimfunga.
. . .

Mama [4]

Si mimi wala Babako
tuliyofunga bali Waislamu
wote wamefunga
Ramadhan [sic]. Elewa
Ramadhani hufungwa. . . .

Typed Copy

Wakati wa Ramadhani mtoto
alianza kumwuliza mama yake
maswali yafuatavyo:

[1] Mtoto: Mama kwa nini ninyi,
wewe na baba mnaonea watoto
kama mimi wakikosa?

[2] Mama: Kwa kweli hatuwaonei
bali ni vitendo vyao hufanya
waonewe na hata kupigwa.

[3] Mtoto: Mbona basi Ramadhani
si mtoto kama mimi na mmesema
mlimfunga?

[4] Mama: Si mimi wala babako
tuliyofunga bali Waislamu wote
wamefunga Ramadhani. Elewa
Ramadhani hufungwa.[2] . . . .

---

[1] The joke original was quite neatly handwritten. I have shown it here in the same spatial layout--only typing it rather than writing it. This joke was typed in the *Baraza* office on November 14, 1972 and probably mailed in several weeks prior to this date. It was printed in the January 25, 1973 column.

[2] For the purposes of this example, it is not necessary to give the complete joke nor the complete translation. The joke is a play upon the phrase *-funga ramadhani*. *Ramadhani* is the Muslim month of fasting, but it is also a common boy's name. *-Funga* means literally to fasten, enclose, imprison. Here the child (*mtoto*) is using the phrase literally to refer to imprisoning a boy named Ramadhani, and the mother (mama) is using it to refer to keeping the fast.

[Numbers in brackets are not part of the originals, but have been added to emphasize the change in arrangement.]

The author of this joke organized the exchange between the characters from left to right across the page, and then down. The secretary has altered this arrangment so that the exchange is organized only down the page.

Original and Printed Jokes

The above example also demonstrates another kind of secretarial editing. In the original written joke there is no lead. In the secretary's version, however, a lead has been supplied for the printer's copy. Several other examples can be given of this kind of editing in which a secretary has altered and/or added to a written joke. This editing may include spelling and grammar. Editing the written jokes which are sent to Baraza is the prerogative of the newspaper, and in all probability jokes which are edited are improved in the process. However, the purpose of this study is best accomplished through the examination of the original written jokes whenever possible. When typographic and composition errors are added to the editing it is clear that the printed joke may not be as useful a document as the original in investigating joke author beliefs.

General Observations of Joke Content

The jokes in the Cheka na Baraza column, of course, are designed to be humorous. Moreover, these jokes do not portray fanciful, improbable, or supernational situations. Some are probably exaggerated in certain ways so as to emphasize the joke's humor, but they are not complete flights of imagination. There are no encounters with supernatural beings or forms, nor, with a few exceptions, talking animals such as in Aesop's fables. The situations depicted in the jokes are based upon ordinary life events. The characters, their actions, and the situations in which they are placed, are all related to real aspects of Kenyan society.

The authors are cognizant of the fact that they are writing to a wide audience. As discussed above, this orientation is also evident in the content of other reader contributions. This means that while joke themes are certainly measured against the author's own experience and understanding of what is humorous, they are not strictly in-group jokes. Even if a joke theme is based upon an in-group experience, it is phrased in such a way as to be understandable to others.[1] In other words, we can assume that these are mostly surface jokes which are not obscure and not dependent upon an insider's understanding of intricate symbolic connotations. The jokes are more probably based upon common experiences of Baraza readers. In addition, the fact that the jokes are written in Swahili is significant because peculiarly in-group meanings must be translated out of the in-group language into Swahili. This sets a limit on the degree to which most jokes can be exclusive.

The Problem of Esoteric Meanings in Joke Content

The analysis of jokes, however, may be subject to a serious obstacle. If the joke is intended to have a meaning that is not necessarily predictable from (normative) context but rather from esoteric, idiosyncratic understanding, then joke context can really never be fixed, and will fluctuate from one author/reader to another

M.M. Abdulaziz, of the University of Nairobi, has supplied an example of this problem in a personal communication. A common joke concerns a situation where a boy and a girl enter a restaurant after meeting on the street and talking in Swahili. The boy orders, in English, "sodas and straws." Whereupon the girl, wanting to show that she, too, knows English, says she "likes to drink sodas and eat

---

[1]This assumption is crucial since one common objection to humor research is that it takes years of intimate experience for an observer to "understand" the full meaning of the humorous productions of a particular group. In a sense this may be true--as it applies to particularly in-group humor. But these are newspaper jokes and, as I have shown for other columns in Baraza, I believe that they are designed to be appreciated by other than fellow in-group members of the authors. This is not to deny that each reader may project his/her own in-group experience into a joke, nor that two readers could laugh for different reasons due to different in-group experiences. It is to say rather that the intent of the author was not to be exclusive.

straws." This joke would seem to be, on its face, a humorous illustration of a language mistake. Abdulaziz, however, upon hearing this joke, stated that in Tanzania the Swahili word for "straws" is mrija and that this word also meant "an exploiter." It seemed to him, therefore, that the point of this joke really was that the boy was hinting to the girl, in English, that he would not pay for her drink.

This is an interpretation that assumes some intention on the part of the joke author, which is not really explicit or obvious to an outsider. The interpretation requires special linguistic knowledge and experience. Certainly any verbal or written utterance can be subjected to a large number of interpretations. The human symbolic ability is powerful enough to enrich and elaborate on the most prosaic and simple statement. Yet it is equally true that humans do not continually, nor even usually, communicate by formulating such involved or intricate meanings.

The joke which Abdulaziz commented on was also one part of a questionnaire on language use which I administered to secondary school students in the Nairobi area.[1] Each student was shown this joke (presented not as a "joke" but as a "situation") and asked to explain what the mistake was in the situation. In a sample of 100 responses, not one student made a reference to the relationship between "straws," mrija, and an "exploiter." These responses instead dealt with the failure of the girl to know what "straws" meant, as well as her desire to "show off" without knowledge, and even the boy's inappropiate switch to English. In effect, the surface content was what the students responded to. And there is no reason to assume any other intention on the part of those who tell or write this joke.

Each joke used in this study has been commented on (and translated) by at least one native Kenyan familiar with a number of Swahili varieties. While this reduces the possible errors which would be present if only the researcher's commentaries were used, it does not

---

[1] This questionnaire is described in more detail in my dissertation "Language Use in Joke Characterization: A Study of Language Stereotypes in Kenya," Syracuse University, 1976.

completely eliminate other explanations. However it does insure that the analyses which follow are at least based upon reasonable or normative assessments of joke content

The Joke Sample

While the Cheka na Baraza column provided the context for the jokes which are the basis of this study, the printed column itself was not an altogether satisfactory place from which to draw a sample of jokes for examination. The printed jokes presented several problems. As already discussed, the printed version may vary in potentially important ways from the original version as prepared by its author. A part of the analysis of the jokes depended upon a careful examination of the written representations of speech in the exchange and the written forms used in the lead. In some cases there may be deliberate changes by joke authors of only one letter. Therefore, it was necessary to examine the original joke and not the printed copy. Second, the printed jokes are anonymous. Some Baraza features give the names and addresses of their contributors, but Cheka na Baraza jokes have always been printed without author name or address. This is a disadvantage because both author's name and address were required for several reasons. An author's address was used to distinguish Kenyan jokes from those sent from Tanzania and Uganda. In addition, authors were to be classed according to their type of residence (or post office box) location as well as their ethnic group. Therefore, this study was limited to an examination of joke originals.

Baraza does not have the office facilities to maintain extensi[illegible] back files of the originals of jokes. As jokes are received in the office, they are placed in a tray to be typed, and then are placed in another tray to await possible selection by staff members for inclusion in the column. If a joke is printed it is filed and periodically a secretary goes through the file to get the names of the authors whose jokes have been printed in order to send them their payments. At indefinite intervals after this, the printed jokes for which payments have been made are disposed of.

[illegible] time, therefore there are probably several hundred jokes in the Baraza offices. These jokes are in various stages of being processed--typed, selected and payed for. I wanted to obtain a large body of joke originals which have been received in a certain time period, but it would have been inconvenient to interrupt the ongoing operations of the newspaper in order to accurately collect and reproduce the joke originals already in the office. One non-disruptive method of collection was to obtain access of jokes soon after they had been delivered to the Baraza offices, before they were processed. I proposed to the Editor that I would sponsor a joke contest by providing a weekly prize for the best joke[1] in return for access to the jokes as they were delivered. In addition to providing access to joke originals, a contest would probably increase the number of jokes submitted. The procedure was to be as follows: The secretary would sort out all joke entries for a week's period starting on Thursday (the day Baraza is published) and at the end of each week I would remove them from the office over the weekend for cataloging. Each author's name and address was recorded with the number of jokes he/she had included in the entry. Some brief notes were made as to joke content. These jokes would be returned and when the secretaries typed the joke copy they would make an extra carbon which I would then, if necessary, conform exactly to the original and keep. In this manner I was able to secure an accurate record of each joke original without interferring with the editorial process.

The joke contest was announced in the April 5 and 12, 1973 issues of Baraza. The following week the Cheka na Baraza column included a winning joke at the head of the column. The contest continued through the June 14, 1973 issue. By following the procedure described above, I was able to collect a total of

---

[1]The sum agreed upon as a reasonable prize was ten shillings (about $1.50). Choosing the best joke each week would be the responsibility of Baraza's staffers. The contest was to run ten weeks, but actually only lasted nine. Readers could send in as many jokes as they wished as often as they liked.

253 jokes from 133[1] Kenya authors.

A representative sample of one joke from each author was selected by the following method. First, jokes were grouped by author's name.[2] Authors were alphabetized (only to provide a convenient listing) and then each author and each joke was assigned a number. One joke from each author was drawn using a table of random numbers. The 133 jokes are the basis for the discussion of speech-based misunderstandings. The first 46 jokes of this sample are reproduced in the Appendix to provide a representative example of the whole joke corpus.

---

[1]The actual total was 148, but the joke entries for 15 authors were misplaced and could not be located.

[2]Most authors submitted only one joke. Some submitted more than one joke, but in each case listed the same name and address. In some cases, jokes whose authors had somewhat different, but similar, names and identical addresses were grouped together--e.g. Rose K. James and Rose Ketty Jim, both from the same post office box, were considered to be the same author.

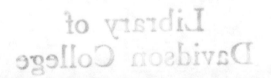

CHAPTER IV: SPEECH-BASED MISUNDERSTANDINGS IN JOKE CONTENT

Many of these jokes depict what I will call "speech misunderstandings." In these jokes the particular form of a character's (or characters') speech is responsible for the humorous misunderstanding which constitutes the point of the joke. In other jokes the speech forms of the characters are not a part of the humorous misunderstanding in the joke--they serve to convey or describe it, but do not cause the misunderstanding itself.

Two examples will serve to illustrate these two kinds of jokes. In the first, joke number 44, there is a misunderstanding involving a literal interpretation of an idiom. (Joke 44 actually depicts two misunderstandings; only the first of these is given here for an example and therefore just the first 20 lines of the joke are used.)

J44:

Mamaake Ali alikuwa mgonjwa sana wa T.B. siku nyingi
na bila kupona. Sasa babaake Ali, akamtuma Ali kupige
Bao kwa mganga ili ajue kiini cha ugonjwa huo.
Baba: Nenda kule ng'ambo ya ule mto ukapige bao
kwa mganga.
Ali: [(]Alikwenda mpaka kwenye Nyumba ya mganga
huku akishikilia gongo mkononi. Akaliona Bao
moja ambalo liko karibu na nyumba ya mganga na
kuanza kulipiga.[)] (mganga mwenyewe alikuwa ndani
ya nyumba. Akasikia bao lake la kakalia huko nje
lapigwa kwa gongo, akatoka nje na kumrukia Ali).
Mganga: Mbona wapiga bao langu hapa nje?
Hujui kwamba utalivunja?
Ali: Baba yangu ameniambia niende kupiga bao
kwa mganga. Na sasa mganga ndio wewe, ndio
maana napiga hili Bao lako.
Mganga: Hapana, yeye hakukwambia uje
upige bao la mti lililo karibu na nyumba yangu.
Mimi najua yeye anataka bao la uganga.
Ali: Basi nifanyie bao la uganga. . . .

In the lead (lines 1-3) we are told that Ali's mother (*mamaake Ali*) has been sick with T.B. [tuberculosis] for many days without improving. Ali's father (*babaake Ali*) sends Ali to have a diviner

(Mganga) consult his divining board (kupiga bao) to determine what should be done about the illness. The misunderstanding which follows is related to the phrase for divining: -piga bao. Bao means a (wooden) board, usually one which has a special purpose such as a chess board or, as in this case, a divining board. -Piga is a verb stem which, by itself, has the primary meaning "to strike, beat, hit, give a blow."[1] But it is also very commonly used to indicate a number of actions, each of which is indicated by the noun following -piga, eg. with kura (dice, lots) -piga kura is "to gamble," with picha (photograph, from the English word picture) -piga picha is "to (make/take a) photograph," and many other combinations. -Piga bao is one of these many combinations and it has the meaning of "divination using a divining board." But literally, it could be interpreted as something like "hit a board," and this is how Ali interprets his father's words. His father tells him to go to the other side of the river and ukapige[2] bao kwa mganga (consult the diviner) (lines 4-5). Ali reaches the diviner's house, begins to beat it (kuanza kulipiga)[3] (line 9). The diviner, who is inside, hears his board being struck and comes outside and jumps at Ali (lead insert, lines 9-11). He asks "why are you hitting my board here outside? Don't you know that you'll break it?" (lines 12-13). Ali answers, "my father told me

---

[1]These meanings are taken from what is, at present, the standard Swahili-English dictionary: The Standard Swahili-English Dictionary (1939) published by Oxford University Press. Whenever a "primary" or "secondary" meaning is referred to in the discussion which follows, it will be based upon this source.

[2]The final -e is probably the subjective suffix which is a more polite command form. I say "probably" only because the -e is used in the lead (line 2) incorrectly with the infinitive prefix ku.

[3]The -li- prefix is the object pronoun for bao. The ku- prefix is the infinitive.

[that] I should come and beat the board of the diviner. Now since you are the diviner, this is the reason why I am hitting your board." (lines 14-16). The diviner replies, "no, he [your father] did not tell you to come and beat a board next to my house. I know he wanted a divination." (lines 17-19).[1] Ali then says, "O.K. perform for me a divination." (line 20), and the joke continues. Instead of using -*piga bao*, Ali here uses a different, somewhat more explicit construction for "divination": *nifanyie* (do/perform for me) *bao la uganga* (a divination, literally a board of divination).

Joke 44 therefore depicts a misunderstanding which is related to speech form--the manner in which something is said. In this case, what is said is a particular idiomatic phrase and the misunderstanding is that the character Ali interprets this phrase literally.

In contrast to Joke 44, Joke 45 does not depict a speech misunderstanding. There is an exchange but although one of the characters is (humorously) misled by what the other character says, the particular forms of speech used are not responsible for the misunderstanding. Speech, in this joke, is essentially neutral.[2]

J45:

Bi Agnes alikuwa akitafuta
mahali pa kukaa ndani ya basi
yenye orofa iliyokuwa imejaa. Kwa
bahati akamwo rafiki yake Wamboi
na wakaanza kuongea.
Agnes: Waenda wapi dada.
Wamboi: Naenda town kununua nguo
Agnes: (Kwa mshangao) Ah! unekosea dada.
teremka kwenye basi
la chini. Hili la juu
linakwenda industrial area (Kwa furaha,
bi Agnes akakaa)

---

[1]The diviner makes this clear by using the phrase *bao la uganga*. The *u*- prefix (instead of *m*) added to the stem -*ganga* indicates the action, or art, of divination.

[2]Related to this "neutrality," and interesting in itself, is the fact that this joke, and jokes like it, are relatively easily translated into English.

Agnes is looking for a place to sit on a crowded bus (basi) which has two levels [a double-decked bus]. By chance she [sees] her friend Wamboi and they start to talk (lead, lines 1-5). Agnes asks where Wamboi is going (using the familiar term of reference among women dada, literally "sister"). Wamboi says that she is going to town to buy clothes. Agnes, with surprise, exclaims, "Why, you have made a mistake 'sister,' get on a single level bus. This double-decked bus is going to the industrial area." (lines 7-11). [Wamboi leaves.] Happily Agnes then sits down [in Wamboi's seat].

Agnes has tricked Wamboi into leaving her seat (and the bus) for her own benefit. The speech of the characters is not directly involved in this deception other than as a medium by which the characters communicate. For the depiction of this situation any kind of speech form would be sufficient (as long as it expressed the same message), eg. this joke could have been just as easily expressed in English or in non-standard Swahili, so long as it would have the same effect.

The exchange in Joke 45, in fact, contains both English and non-standard Swahili forms. In line 7, Wamboi is dipected as using the English "town" instead of the Swahili mji, and in line 11 Agnes uses "industrial area" instead of (perhaps) mahali pa utendaji. Neither of these English forms has an effect upon Agnes' trick nor Wamboi's deception. Agnes also uses the English loan basi (bus, line 9). This is an established loan, and has been modified to conform to Swahili phonology by the addition of the final vowel; still, it is a foreign loan. However, its presence also has no effect upon the situation. Agnes' Swahili is marked in one place by a non-standard form (possibly one caused by vernacular interference). In line 9, she uses teremka instead of the standard telemka ("get off, down").[1] Standard Swahili distinguishes between /r/ and /l/, but many vernaculars do not and the incorrect

---

[1]This form is probably a result of the joke author's own first language interference.

substitution of one sound for the other is a common form of interference in Swahili. Regardless, the presence of teremka also has no obvious effect upon the joke situation. All of these non-standard forms may be necessary components of the characterization in the joke, but they are not a necessary part of the joke situation.

There is one possible objection to the foregoing conclusion about the function of the speech depiction in Joke 45, and this should be dealt with. It could be argued that the speech forms depicted in the exchange are in fact directly related to the joke. The presence of English words might be deliberately used to mark both as "educated" women and thus the cleverness of Agnes and the gullibility of Wamboi might therefore be of a more humorous nature. It is undeniably true that characterization, through speech as well as by character labels and description, is directly related to joke situations. But there is a significant difference between Jokes 45 and 44 in regard to the manner in which speech form is used in the joke. In Joke 45 the particular speech forms which are depicted for Agnes and Wamboi may indeed, as an integral part of their characterization, heighten the humor of the joke situation. But they do not themselves create the joke situation by being a source of misunderstanding, confusion, or some other failure or error of communication. Agnes and Wamboi communicate very well. In Joke 46, on the other hand, Ali and his father have communicated very badly in the sense that Ali has interpreted his father's words literally and consequently does a foolish act. Aside from Ali's lack of knowledge, and/or his foolishness, his comincal behavior can be related to the particular forms of his father's words. -Piga bao can be literally interpreted as "beat a board," as well as interpreted idiomatically as "divination."

In jokes of J45's type, speech form is not a completely neutral (or unconscious) medium of communication. Rather, speech becomes involved as a part of the communication itself by presenting barriers either through the way in which speech forms are produced, and/or through the way in which they are received. In these jokes speech and language becomes part of the object of the joke situation. The types of jokes will be examined next in regard to the way in which they depict certain kinds of speech misunderstandings.

The Depiction of Speech Misunderstandings Based Upon Semantic Elaboration of Swahili

This communicational difficulty is related both to the expansion of Swahili's role in national affairs, and to the semantic elaboration which is associated with its communicational development. This potential barrier to efficient communication is caused by what Whiteley calls an overly heavy "connotational load" on single Swahili lexemes (1969:120). Whiteley's example of this condition is the heavy semantic weight carried by the form uchumi which has been elaborated through the development of western economic terminology in Swahili and now has at least five technical economic meanings, as described previously. Whiteley's point is that this kind of homonym is not efficient for conducting a nation's technical business. Although Whiteley does not present many other examples of this problem, nor illustrate how uchumi's connotational load actually causes inefficient communication, he does make a plausible point.[1] Homonyms exist in all natural languages, and it is certainly probable that many of these would exist in speech environments that are similar enough (if not

---

[1]Whiteley is generally referrring to the use of Swahili terms in Tanzania with this example. However, this kind of semantic elaboration is not unusual and could also occur for Kenyans.

identical) for confusion to result through resultant ambiguity. However, if Swahili, as Whiteley suggests, has developed a large number of homonyms which, like uchumi, are all of the same grammatical class (so that they would occur in similar structural environments--eg. unafikiri juu ya uchumi, "you are thinking about _____________"), then the potential for confusion is present. This potential confusion would be greatly heightened if, like uchumi, all the meanings of these homonyms were closely related within the same semantic domain.[1]

Jokes Depicting Misunderstandings Due to Semantic Elaboration

In Joke 1, the misunderstanding is based upon a significant difference between a "literal" (or primary meaning) of a phrase and a newer idiomatic meaning.

J1:

Siku moja Onyango alikwenda mjini kutafuta kazi, mara akaingia ndani ya duka la Patel na kuuliza kazi.
Onyango: Jambo mitu ya Banglades.
Patel: Jambo bana Africa.
Onyango: Banakoba mimi nataka kasi.
Patel: Ooooh! Veve kaji taka.
Onyango: Ndio misee.
Patel: Veve makono ako refu fupi?
Onyango: Ooowi! mikono yangu mirefu Bwana.
Patel: Oooh Bagwan! Chori kusa kuja, veve sema makono alo refu, mimi pantaka wewe iko miji kuba!
Onyango: Mimi apana iko mitu ya miji mimi olitoka U.K.!

Capsule translation--
Onyango goes into town looking for work. He enters Patel's shop. Patel asks him if he is trustworthy

---

[1] It could be argued that humor involving homonyms and multiple meanings (e.g. puns) is more effective when the confused meanings are in widely separate domains. Koestler (1964), for example, in his concept of "bisociation" claims that the greater the "gap" between the meanings, the greater tension there is to be relieved in laughter. While not denying the validity of this approach, I will not accept it as a necessary feature of these jokes. Insofar as there is any marked difference in meaning--as opposed to the slight difference among synonyms, I will assume that it may be the basis of a joke.

(literally, are his hands long or short--'long hands' meaning a thief). Onyango does not understand, and wanting to please, responds that his hands are long. Patel exclaims that he doesn't want a thief in town and Onyango says he is not from town but from "U.K." [United Kisumu--a Luo area].

Onyango has gone to the city, to Patel's shop, asking for work. The shopkeeper, Patel asks Onyango if he has makono ako refu fupi? (line 8). Literally this would mean "are your arms long or short," and Onyango replies to this interpretation by stating that his arms are long--mikono yangu mirefu (line 9). Onyango's response is appropriate given the literal meaning of Patel's question. But Patel is using a modern idiom and is asking if Onyango is honest and "having long arms" is an idiom for dishonesty among store clerks.

It is important to note that Onyango's misunderstanding is not apparently due to Patel's varietal Swahili. Patel is simply depicted as using his non-standard variety of Swahili and asking what is for him an appropriate question. Onyango could very well have been depicted as being misled by the form of Patel's speech but rather he was misled by his own lack of understanding of the alternate meaning.

In Joke 12, the misunderstanding arises from the difference between the older meaning of makaa (charcoal) and a newer meaning--"batteries."

J12:

Eliud alimtuma baba yake amununulie betri za Radio na akamwambia anunue makaa ya Radio.
Eliud: Baba ni wakati gani utaenda Madukani nikutume?
Baba: Hata sasa niko naondoka.
Eliud: Basi hizi pesa ununue makaa ya Everedy. (Baba akafika kwa duka la Joswa).
Baba: Nipe makaa.
Joswa: Zunguka nyuma uyachague.
Baba: Gunia ni bei gani?
Joswa: Shilingi tano. (Baba akapeleka gunia la makaa nyumbani).
Eliud: Mbona hukuyanunua makaa yaa Radio niliyo-kutuma?
Baba: Si ulisema ninunue makaa hii.

Eliud: Hukusikia vizuri nilisema ya Radio, rudi tena umwambie mwenye duka akupe betri nyekundu za Radio.

Baba: Ooh! Ulisema ile betri nyekundu? nina-ijua mbona hukusema betri ukasema makaa. Akiba haiozi tutaota hii.

Capsule translation--
Eliud sends his father to get "makaa" [meaning batteries] for his radio but the father comes back with charcoal ["makaa" also means charcoal] which he bought at Joswa's store. When the son asks why, the father replies that he should have said that he wanted batteries, "betri", and anyway the charcoal will be used.

Eliud asks his father to buy makaa ya Everedy (line 6). Makaa means "charcoal" and this is what the father buys at the store and brings home (lines 7-12). But Eliud is using makaa to mean "batteries." There is an English loan word available "betri" (which the father knows and uses in line 20) but instead Eliud uses makaa with this modern meaning. It is interesting to note here that it is not the English loan betri but the elaboration of makaa which causes the confusion.

In Joke 27, the misunderstanding is based upon the difference between a literal and a new idiomatic meaning of a phrase:

J27:

Baba mmoja baada ya kushoshwa na tabia mbaya za mwanawe alianza kumshauri ili aache kutenda maovu lakini palitokea zogo kali baina yao hata mtoto akazidi kumkasirisha sana babake wakati alipojaribu kumwambia hivi:

BABA: Usipoyashika haya yangu na kuacha kujichukulia sheria mikononi siku moja utakiona kilichomnyoa kanga manyoya.

MTOTO: Mimi sijachukua sheria yeyote mikononi wala sinayo kabisa mifukoni!!!

Capsule translation--
Father is lecturing child on bad behavior. Child becomes angry when father says that he shouldn't take the "sheria" [law] into his own hands. Child replies that he hasn't taken any "sheria" in his hands nor in his pocket.

The father (baba) tells his ill-mannered son that he shouldn't "take the law into his own hands"--kujichukulia sheria mikononi (line 7). The son interprets this literally rather than as a new, European-derived idiom and (possibly because he also does not know the meaning of sheria "law" and thinks it means some kind of thing) responds that he hasn't taken (stolen) any sheria in his hands, or his pockets.

Joke 46 provides an example of a misunderstanding involving an alternate meaning of a brand name:

J46: Mamo mmoja alimtuma mwanawe Ali kwenye duka la viatu vya bata akanunue viatu, Nyumbani mlikuwa na bata mzinga. Mambo yakawa hivi:

Mama: Ali.
Ali: Ee mama.
Mama: Shika hizi shilingi hamsa ishirini ukanunue viatu vya bata.
Ali: Ati umesema ni hamsa ishirini mama?
Mama: Ndio.
Ali: Hizo zote, shilingi sabini ni za viatu vya bata?
Mama: Shika nenda haraka sana.
Ali: Ah! mama hizi ni ishirini na tano tu, si sabini.
Mama: Shukua hizo ukimbie haraka.
Ali: Habari mwenye duka.
Mwenye duka: Nzuri
Ali: Mimi nataka viatu vya bata, unazo?
Mwenye duka: Ndio wataka namba ngapi na rangi gani?
Ali: Sikumwuliza mama bata wetu huvaa namba ngapi wala rangi?
Mwenya duka: Ni vyako au ni yva bata?
Ali: Hebu niende kumpima bata wetu nione ni namba ngapi atavaa na rangi gani.
Mwenye duka: Subiri kidogo, mimi huuza viatu vinavyo tengenezwa na kampuni ya bata wala si viatu vya bata.

Capsule translation--
Ali is sent by his mother to buy some "Bata" shoes [a brand of shoe; also means duck]. When the shoe salesman asks for size and color, Ali says he doen't know what size the ducks need nor what color they would like. The salesman says we sell Bata shoes not shoes for ducks.

A mother (mama) sends her son Ali to a Bata [brand] shoe store (duka la viatu vya bata) to buy shoes (lead, line 1). They also have ducks (bata) at their house. Ali does not understand brand names and interprets his mother's request literally as meaning that he should buy shoes for the ducks. At the store, when the owner (mwenye duka) asks for size and color (namba ngapi na rangi gani, line 19), Ali says he really does not know and he must go and measure the ducks (line 23-24). Brand names employing standard Swahili words are an obvious western introduction and source of semantic elaboration. There are animal names for many products, yet this is the only joke dealing with this topic. It can be compared with a similar misunderstanding involving football team names (Joke 98, shown below, page 52).

In Joke 51 the misunderstanding is related to ordering tea in a restaurant and the double meaning of the phrase chai bure.

J51:

Abdullah baada ya kufika Kisumu kutoka mkoa wa Pwani, alingia hoteli moja kwa kujiburudisha na kinywaji. Mtumishi moja jina Odhiambo alienda mezani ku muuliza kitu alietaka. Mambo yalikuwa kama ifwatavyo:

Odhiambo: Misawe Omera.
Abdullah: Sema nini wewe? Kwani kila mtu mji huu ni kabila yako?
Odhiambo: Oh sole memi ne lefikiri wewe ne jeluo.
Abdullah: Haya sema ki swahili.
Odhiambo: Hojambo sana obwana mokobwa.
Abdullah: Sijambo sana bwana mdogo.
Odhiambo: Wewe onataka neni hapa?
Abdullah: Nataka chai.
Obhiambo: Onataka chai bure?
Abdullah: Yaah naweza kufarahi sana kupata chai bure.
Odhiambo: Haya nimeleta chai heyo konywa.
Abdullah: Utanipatia vikombe ngapi via chai?
Odhaimbo: Wewe endelea konywa kepemo onataka.
Abdullah: Mimi hutumia vikombe via chai inne pekee yako tu.
Odhiambo: Wewe abana endelea konywa chai?
Abdullah: Nimeshashiba Ahsante sana kwa kunikaribisha.
Odhiambo: Bei ya kukombe moja ni peni mbeli na ndololo sasa yote ni silinji meja.
Abdullah: Allah! Si uliniambia chai ni ya bure?
Odhiambo: Wolololo! Mimi obana omwambia wewe namna heyo memi omwambia onataka chai na tosti au bure.
Abdullah: Ki swahili yako mpovu kabisa. Si ungeniulize ikiwa nilitaka chai pekee yake au chai bila kitu ngine?
Odhiambo: Wewe Obana kojoa ke swahili ngomu bwana.
Abdullah: Basi shiga pesa zake hizo, kwa heri.
Odhiambo: O kwaheri O kwa onona.

Capsule translation--
Abdullah arrives in Kisumu from the coast and stops to

> have tea. At first he is greeted by the waiter Odhiambo in Luo [Kisumu is in a Luo area] and he objects, asking if everyone is Luo here. He then asks for tea and Odhiambo asks him if he wants *chai bure*. One standard meaning of *bure* is "free" and so Abdullah agrees to what he thinks is free tea. But *bure* in the restaurant means "without toast" and misled by this change in meaning Abdullah must pay for four cups.

Abdullah, who is from the coast, has arrived in Kisimu on the shore: of Lake Victoria. He enters a *hoteli* (cafe or tea stall) to get something to drink and is greeted by the waiter (*mtumishi*) Odhiambo Abdullah requests tea (*nataka chai*; line 13) and Odhiambo asks, "*Onataka chai bure*" (standard: *unataka* . . ., line 14). Literally this would mean free tea since *bure* is an adverb meaning "gratis, for nothing." Here, however, it means tea without any other food as Odhiambo explains in line 27--"*chai na tosti au bure*" (tea with toast or without [toast]). Abdullah pays for what he had thought was going to be free, but he tells Odhiambo that his Swahili is bad and that he should have said "*chai pekee yake au chai bila kitu ngine*" (tea by itself or tea without another thing, lines 29-30). Abdullah's Swahili is not 'good' Swahili either, it should be noted, and his statement would better be written as *chai ya pekee yake* or *chai bila kitu kiingine*. It is true, as Abdullah says, that Odhiambo's Swahili is not standard but the fault really lies with the new (perhaps local) restaurant meaning of *bure*.

Joke 82 is, in some respects, similar to Joke 51 in that both involve a misunderstanding of restaurant terms:

J82:

Onyango, Otieno na Ondieki wamefika Mombasa Kutoka Kisumu kwa transifa. Wakaingie kwa hoteli moja ili wajipatie chakula.
Waiter: Semeni wanainchi, Mumeisha agiza chakula?
Customer: Brother, Niletee chai china.
Waiter: CHAI CHINA, CHAI CHINA MOYA.
Waiter kwa Onyango!: Nawewe Rafiki?

---

[1] A preliminary confusion results from Odhiambo's use of a Luo greeting (line 5) because he thinks Abdullah is also Luo. Abdullah asks him to speak Swahili (line 9) and Odhiambo continues in interference-marked Swahili. But Odhiambo's Swahili variety is not the cause of the joke misunderstanding.

Onyango: Mimi neletee yeye CHAI INDIA, au kama yeye apana yiko, leteya yeye CHAI U.K.
Waiter: Loo! Hiyo unasema bwana hatuna.
Onyango: Yiko ya china peke yake?
Waiter: Afande bwana.
Onyango: Okey, Leteya yeye ugali na nyama na supu yake mizuri.
Waiter: Nyama gani bwana?
Onyango: Nyama ya ng'ombe emekwisha chijwa na supu yake.
Waiter: "Sima moya na ngombe karanga, Sima moya na ngombe karanga."
Waiter kwa Otieno na Ondieki: Nanyinyi wanainhi?
Otieno: Mimi vile vile neletee mimi kama hiyo.
Ondieki: Nyama ya kuku, supu ya kuku imekwisha chijwa na chapati mumoja mukubwa.
Waiter anakuja mbiu na chakula: "china kwa nani, Nani ngombe?" akaweka ng'ombe kwa Onyango- "Wewe ng'ombe"
Onyango: Ee! Mimi ng'ombe na wewe kondo bibi.
Waiter: Hapana bwana nelisema tu hiyo nyama yako ya ng'ombe.
Onyango: Tena nasema nyama yangu ya ng'ombe. Wewe nataka nikupige nashahani? Mimi binadamu, pana nyama ya ng'ombe.
Otieno: Rafiki niletee suruali.
Waiter: Naam bwana.
Otieno: Leteya yeye supu.
Waiter: Ooo! NG'OMBE SURWA, NG'OMBE SURWA.

Capsule translation--
Onyango, Otieno, and Ondieke arrive in Mombasa from Kisumu and enter a restaurant to eat. Onyango is confused first by a customer saying chai china [intended meaning not known but probably a kind of tea] and he thinks this means tea from China. After ordering nyama ya ng'ombe [beef, lit. meat of a cow], he is insulted when the waiter brings it and asks, in a manner of Western waiters, wewe ng'ombe, meaning "did you order beef?" but literally "you [are] a cow," which is a standard insult. [The rest of the joke is not clear.]

Onyango, Otieno and Ondieki have arrived in Mombasa from Kisumu. Just the reverse of the situation in Joke 51. They enter a hoteli (cafe or tea stall) to get some food. Onyango hears a customer ask for "chai china" (line 5), and, interpreting this to mean "Chinese tea," asks for Indian tea ("chai India," line 8) or British tea ("chai U.K." [United Kingdom], line 9).[1] The waiter

[1] "Chai china" is probably an idiom for a form of tea (such as tea with cream and sugar). My informants were not clear on its meaning, and one even made the same interpretation as Onyango by giving it the meaning of Chinese tea.

says, "that which you have said we do not have" (*Hiyo unasema bwana hatuna,* line 10). A second misunderstanding occurs after they place their orders for food--Onyango asks for beef, porridge and meat "*Nyama ya ng'ombe* (line 16; literally, "meat of a cow". When the waiter hurriedly brings the food he says to Onyango "*Wewe ng'ombe*" (literally, "you [are a] cow," line 24). The waiter means "you [are the one who ordered] cow,"[1] but Onyango thinks he is being insulted since calling someone a cow (*ng'ombe*) is a common insult. The waiter apologizes by explaining what he really meant (line 26) and they go on with their meal.

Joke 98 involves a double misunderstanding over sport idioms involving two football (soccer) teams named Mamba (crocodile) and *Simba* (lion).

J98:

Mture: Ewe bwana Kibene, Wiki hii kivumbi. Mamba kameza Simba mara mbili!

Kibene: Aa Mamba awezaje kummeza Simba mara mbili?

Mture: Mbona huelewi. Sisemi simba na mamba wanyama bali Timu ya mpira ya Mamba iliifunga ile ya Simba mara mbili wiki hii.

Capsule translation--
Mture tells Kibene that there was trouble this week, that *Mamba kameza Simba* [literally: "Crocodile swallowed Lion"] twice. [In the modern sport idiom this refers to the team named *Mamba* defeating the team *Simba* twice.] Taking the literal, standard meaning, Kibene expresses disbelief and Mture then explains what he meant by his statement.

The first character, Mture, tells the second, Kibene, that "*Mamba kameza Simba mara mbili*" (the Mamba/crocodile [team] swallowed the *Simba*/lion [team] twice, lines 1-2). Kibene asks how is a crocodile able to swallow a lion twice and Mture explains that he meant that the football team (*timu ya mpira*, line 5) Mamba defeated (*iliifunga*, line 5) *Simba*. This is a dual misunderstanding because both the use of the term for "swallow" meaning "defeat" and the presence of animal-named teams are modern extensions of standard

[1] The waiter's verbal behavior is very much like (if not based upon) the manner of an American counter man asking the customer who had ordered the fish dinner plate, "Hey Mac; are you the fish?"

Swahili words. (This joke should be compared with Joke 46 involving brand names, above pages 48-49.)

In Joke 101 there is a misunderstanding about a bottle (of beer) between a customer in a bar, Ngoroma, and the waiter:

J101:

Ngoroma alikwenda kwa bar akiwa na nia ya kunywa bia moja, na mambo yakawa hivi:
Ngoroma: Nipe chupa moja waiter. baridi rakini.
Waiter: (Huku akimletea chupa tupu ya bia, rakini atuna ya baridi mana yake atuweki chupa tupu kwa barafu.)
Ngoroma: Alaa wee una wasimu? wewe waiter wa upande gani? nilikuambia uniletee bia wa unanipa chupa tupu.
Waiter: (Huku akicheka) rakini ulisema nikupe chupa moja na sisi atuusi chupa tupu tunausa bia, ata mimi nilishangaa rakini nakaona lazima nikuretee ulichokuwa ukikitaka.

Capsule translation--
Ngoroma enters a bar to drink a beer but when he orders he asks only for a cold bottle. The waiter interprets this literally and brings an empty bottle (not cold since they do not keep empty bottles in the refrigerator). Ngoroma is taken aback, but the waiter tells him that he only ordered a bottle, not a beer, and although he [the waiter] was surprised he brought what he wanted.

Ngoroma enters a bar to drink a beer (bia) and so tells the waiter "Bring me one bottle" (*Nipe chupa moja*, line 3). The waiter brings him an empty bottle (*chupa tupu*, line 4). When Ngoroma complains the waiter laughs and tells him that he [Ngoroma] asked for "one bottle" and that since they sell beer, not empty bottles, he was surprised but he necessarily brought what he [Ngoroma] wanted. In this joke, it is the customer who uses a modern idiom, and not the waiter as in Joke 51 (above pages 49-50) and Joke 82 (above pages 50-51).

Joke 109 depicts a misunderstanding over the Christian idiom "Love your neighbor":

J109:

Kiplangat ameokolewa kwa Jina la Yesu
Kwa hiyo hakosi kuhudhuria misa na mafunzo
ya kidini siku moja baada ya kutoka kanisani
alikutana na rafiki ya Otieno na maneno
yakawa hivi:

Kiplangat: Mimi ligua na gwenda Kanisani na
Padri na fundisha mimi
atinipende jirana yangu kama
rafiki yangu
Otieno: Ni kweli bwana Kiplangat
onapenda jirani yako namna ibo.
Kiplangat: Ndiyoo mimi napenda binti yako.
Otieno: (kwa hasira) Serious olifundishwa
atiopende binti yangu pekee kama
onachesa mimi tanyorosa kabisa
mpaka ojue ati ni jaluo otaki
macheso ya atongo yako na
mungu yako hiyo.
Kiplangat: Nihusumie hiyo si lugha
Uchanja yangu tuu.

Capsule translation--
Kiplangat was converted to Christianity and after church one day he meets his friend Otieno. Kiplangat says that the Padri taught him to love his neighbor as his friend. Otieno asks if he loves his neighbor and Kiplangat says that he loves Otieno's daughter. Otieno becomes angry and tells Kiplangat that if he 'plays' he will be beaten. Kiplangat apologizes [saying that the language is not his].

Kiplangat has become a Christian, ameololewa kwa Jina la Yesu (saved through the name of Jesus, line 1), and does not fail to attend mass and learn about the teachings of the religion. When he meets his friend Otieno he tells him that he has been taught that he should love his neighbor as his friend--nipende jirana[i] langu kama rafiki yangu (lines 8-9). The verb -penda (here in the subjunctive form -pende) meaning "love, like" probably expresses the Christian idiom fairly well. However, when Kiplangat illustrates the expression more specifically in reference to Otieno's daughter (binti) saying mimi napenda binti yako (I love your daughter, line 12), Otieno interprets this literally as a sexual reference (as -penda would be used of a man for a woman) and he angrily warns Kiplangat that if he 'plays around' he will be beaten.

Joke 127 is about the practice of restaurants using abbreviated descriptions for their entrees, and in this respect it is similar to Joke 82. Here, however, the misunderstanding is partly based on a written form, and the effect of the misunderstanding is different:

J127:

Wanjiru ilikuwa siku ya kwanza kwenda
Mahoteli makubwa makuwba, akaingia moja
ili apate cha saa sita. Akasoma bei ya
vyakula akaona. Ngombe-----3.00
Wanjiru: Lete ngombe moja.
Mtumishi: Ngombe moja shilingi tatu.
Wanjiru: Sijui kama nitamaliza ngombe
moja.
Mtumishi: Sasa nilete nusu.
Wanjiru: Shilingi moja na thumuni.
Ntumishi: Ndiyo mama.
Wanjiru: Kata kati-kati unileteе upande
wa nyuma yenye sitaki
Mtumishi: (akaleta) ndiyo hii mama.
Wanjiru: he! he! he! nilifikiri
nilakula na kubeba nyingine
kwa kikapu.

Capsule translation--
Wanjiru goes into a large [European-type] hotel [restaurant] for the first time to have dinner. She sees a sign: Ng'ombe ... 3.00 (Beef ... 3 shillings). She tells the waiter she wants one cow but then decides that, since she couldn't finish a whole cow, she will have a half. She tells the waiter to cut it in half. When he brings it to her [a half of a piece of meat] she exclaims that she thought that she would be able to eat and still carry the rest home.

Wanjiru goes into one of the big restaurants (mahoteli makubwa makubwa [reduplication of adjective -kubwa "large"], line 2) and and sees a sign "Ngombe [sic][1] -----3.00" (cow-----3.00 [shillings]). The word ng'ombe refers to the animal and the term nyama (meat) must be used as a qualifier in standard Swahili to refer to a cut of the carcass. However, restaurants have developed a new meaning for ng'ombe by listing it on menus by itself meaning the meat, or "beef." Wanjiru, however, thinks that this means a whole cow and tells the waiter to bring her half (nusu). When he brings her the meat [a half portion], she exclaims "I thought I will eat and carry the rest in my basket" (lines 15-17).

---

[1]The standard orthographic representation for cow is ng'ombe. The diacritic after "ng" indicates that this is a velar nasal stop and not a combination of an "n" and a "g". This omission is not significant in this joke.

Absence of Stereotypes Concerning Speech Misunderstandings Due to Semantic Elaboration in Technical Domains

One conclusion is immediately apparent; contrary to what might be expected according to Whiteley, these jokes do not depict misunderstandings which are based upon the elaboration of Swahili into technical semantic domains. None of the jokes involves governmental, economic, business, or industrial affairs. Instead, the semantic elaboration involves brand names, football team names, restaurant idioms and the creation of (non-technical) Swahili idioms after English patterns (e.g. "Take the law into your hands").

Whiteley, whose assessment of Swahili's semantic elaboration formed the basis of this examination, was primarily referring to the situation in Tanzania. In Kenya, however, Swahili's development into the English-dominated domains of science, industry, and national affairs began very late. It seems reasonable to assume that the kind of misunderstanding alluded to by Whiteley does not appear in Kenyan jokes because this kind of upward elaboration of Swahili into technical domains has not yet been achieved. Conversely, it is equally apparent that if Swahili has not (yet) moved into the domains of economics and technology dominated by English usage, it has at least responded semantically to the Westernization of Kenyan life.

The Depiction of Speech Misunderstandings Based Upon Phonological and Grammatical Interference in Spoken Swahili

In sixteen jokes one, or both, of the joke characters produces a Swahili-based utterance which creates a speech misunderstanding because of its phonological or grammatical deviation from the form of standard Swahili. Swahili is primarily spoken in Kenya as a second language, and this status is revealed in the presence and use of interference-marked varieties of Swahili (hereafter called IMV Swahili). Here, the depiction of IMV Swahili will be examined in relation to its role in causing speech misunderstandings.

Joke characters are often depicted in the exchange speaking Swahili which is marked by phonological or grammatical interference. A character might say, for example (in Joke 29, line 3: shown below) thiku instead of the standard siku, thereby being depicted as producing an initial dental, or interdental, fricative rather than the standard alveolar fricative).[1] Or, a character might say (in Joke 84, line 3; see page 72) wapi taa instead of the standard taa iko wapi (where is the light) thereby being depicted as producing an ungrammatical word order and omitting iko, the locative form of the copula.

Speech Misunderstandings, Interlocutors, and Message Predictability

Before describing these sixteen jokes several observations must be made concerning speech misunderstandings caused by IMV Swahili.

That these jokes exist at all is not particularly remarkable. It would, in fact, be much more surprising if there were no such jokes from a country as linguistically heterogeneous as Kenya. As a second language, Swahili is inevitably subject to some variability due to vernacular interference. Further, the existence of many different vernaculars (including English), and correspondingly the presence of different kinds of IMV Swahili, should ensure that at least some of this variation is readily apparent to most (if not all) users of Swahili. However, the use of phonological and grammatical interference as the basis for speech misunderstandings in these jokes is only developed to a limited extent.

Sixteen of 133 jokes depict this type of misunderstanding. This proportion cannot, by itself, be assessed as large or small, since there are no comparative data against which to measure it. It is important to note, however, that there are many jokes in which characters successfully communicate despite their use of IMV Swahili. The sixteen jokes of this section have been examined as if they constituted a separate group representing a body of shared

---

[1]A major assumption is that even though non-standard speech variations are being depicted, they are being depicted in accordance with standard orthography--e.g. the sound represented by the graph "th" is an interdental, voiceless fricative and not, for example, an aspirated dental stop. The standard forms of orthography are here all based upon the Standard Swahili-English Dictionary.

beliefs about the communicational efficiency of spoken, varietal Swahili. As an illustration of the factors to be considered in examining the manner in which varietal Swahili may be misinterpreted, I will describe a joke which depicts the use of varietal Swahili without a misunderstanding.

Joke 18 (shown in the Appendix) depicts a conversation between an Indian (Baniani) and his driver, Kiplangat. The conversation is marked by speech forms such as the Indian's dengenecha (standard: -tengeneza, to mend) or alavu (standard: halafu, afterwards), and Kiplangat's ukali (standard: ugali, porridge) or masiwa (standard: maziwa, milk), yet none of these forms are misunderstood. There are two interrelated reasons why no speech misunderstanding should be expected to occur.

The first reason is that, as employer and employee (rather than two strangers), the two characters are presumably used to each other's speech. Any speech, in IMV as well as Standard Swahili, can be understood if the hearer is used to it. The second reason is that (some of) the messages being communicated are predictable. The Indian's instructions to Kiplangat on what to do with the car and the food could have been mumbled, or, even granting that Kiplangat was not familiar with his employer's speech, spoken with phonological deviation and still have been communicated. In fact, if there were to be a misunderstanding, according to this aspect of communication, it should have been when Kiplangat responded that he did not want to eat the Indian's (spicy) food. This message was surely not expected, but even so it is understood by the Indian. That this "unexpected" message was successfully transmitted by Kiplangat's IMV Swahili means that the Indian would be used to decoding his driver's speech forms.

In some circumstances, therefore, phonological (and grammatical) variation need not necessarily be a barrier to communication. Friends, family members, certain employees and their employers, would be sufficiently familiar with each other's speech to decode speech variations. If the speech message(s) are expected, or readily predictable, the effect of phonological and/or grammatical variations should be negligible. If speech variation does create confusion, it should do so in situations where the interlocutors are not familiar with each other and are transmitting new or unpredictable messages.

Jokes Depicting Misunderstandings Based upon IMV Swahili

In the presentation which follows, jokes involving only phonological-based misunderstandings are given first (ending with Joke 129, page 67, followed by jokes involving grammatical-based misunderstandings.

In Joke 15, the speech misunderstanding is related to the standard form kodi (tax) being said as kothi and then being heard as koti (coat):

J15:

Bwana Mramba alikutana na Bwana Marua asikari
na mambo yakawa hiivi:
Marua ako simama:
Mramba mimi:
asikari [Marua] ndio wewe kwani iko mthuingine:
Mramba [(]alisimama[)]
Marua [(]alipofikal)] unakwenda-wapi:
[Mramba] nakwenda nyumbani.
[(]maana-ikuwa saatatu usiku[)]
asikari [Marua] wewe nikuwa narara wapi
Mramba nyumbaya-ngu iko Majengo ndikonilalako
asikari [Marua] thoakothi
Mramba [(]anatoa koti alilo vaa:[)]
asikari Marua unatoa kothi gani una thaka
kunipika?
Mramba [(]akalishwa kofi na kusema [)] ki kwao
(ala! mbonawe)
Marua: Una thukana mimi [(]akamlisha lingine
nakutia mkono mfukoni ambamo alipata
chetichakodi alimrudishi naku mpa-
teke aka mwambia [)] kwenda na ha pana
angaria nyuma.
[(]mbonawe (vipi wewe)[)].

Capsule translation--
One evening, Mr. Mramba is stopped by Policeman Marua. Marua asks for Mramba's "kothi" [tax receipt--standard form is Kodi], but Mramba gives him his "koti" [coat]. Matua kicks Mramba, checks his tax papers and tells him to go.

In line 12, Marua the policeman ("asikari," standard: askari) says "thoakothi" (show [your] tax [receipt], standard: toa kodi) but the other character, Mramba, instead shows his coat (toa koti, line 13).[1] The officer's pronunciation of kodi as kothi misleads Mramba into thinking that it is his coat that is wanted and causes him, as the joke proceeds, to receiving a beating for his error.

In Joke 32 there is a misunderstanding about the work jua (sun), in the phrase sun glasses, which is pronounced as chua:

J32:

Oiro alinunua mewani ya chua, Fred alipo-
muona amevaa mazunguzo yao yakawa hivi
Oiro- Jana nilienda kwa duka fulani
nikanunua mewani hii ya chua.
Fred- Ulinunua ya chua namna gani?
Oiro- Nilinua ya chua kwa sababu macho
yangu hasioni vizuri wakati wa chua.
Fred- Yaani hufahamu neno chua, chua
ni mtu mpumbavu, ama ulinunua
kutoka kwa mtu mpumbavu?
Oiro- La, nilinua kutoka kwa duka fulani
ukinunua mewani ya chua utakuwaje
mpumbavu.

Capsule translation--
Orio has bought sun-glasses and when he tells Fred about buying these glasses [mewani hii] for the sun [ya chua, standard: miwani hii ya jua], Fred interprets chua as juha [fool] and asks are they a fool's glasses or did you buy them from a fool.

Orio tells Fred about buying his sun-glasses but pronounces the word for sun as chua instead of the standard jua (lines 4, 6, and 2). Fred responds as though Oiro had said "fool" (standard: juha) by telling Oiro that chua means a foolish person (chua ni

[1]This joke is particularly difficult to analyze because it is one of those few jokes which are prepared in a format quite different from that used in the Cheka na Baraza column. One difference is that character names are not set off from their speech and parts of the lead are not distinguished from parts of the exchange. This phrase in line 13 is standard, but is part of a lead insert telling what the character did, not what he said. Necessary clarifications are added in brackets.

mtu mpumbavu, lines 8-9).[1]

In Joke 36 there is a misunderstanding concerning the word miguu (legs) pronounced as miku:

J36:

James alikuwa anaenda shuleni aka
pata Mzee shem anangoja basi
lakumtuba taoni Basi mambo yakawa hivi:
James- Jambo Mzee
Mzee shem- Jambo Kijana.
James- Unatabu gani Mzee
Shem- Mimi naongoja basi niende
taoni. Kwa vile mimi naona
nimbali sana siwezi fika hu
ko namiku.
Jamesi- Tuseme Ukipata Basi Utawa
ja miku hapa Mzee.
Shem- wewe ahuna adabu una
soma wapi wewe mtoto bumb
afu namna hii
James- Mimi nasoma kwa kitabu.

Capsule translation--
James on his way to school, sees an old man Shem waiting and asks him what he is doing. Shem says he is waiting for a bus to town because it is too far to "fika huko namiku" (get there on foot, standard: . . . na miguu) (lines 10-11). James interprets namiku as meaning "with miku" and so asks if he will leave the miku here [it is not clear what James thinks miku is].

In lines 10 and 11, Shem tells James fika huko namiku meaning "arrive on foot." The form na is a general purpose particle that can be used to indicate an agent of an action, as Shem uses it in namiku to mean "on foot" (standard: na miguu). Na can also indicate connection or association, e.g. "with," and this is how James interprets namiku--that Shem is going with something called a miku. This last is the phonological basis for the misunderstanding since

---

[1] This depiction of a speech misunderstanding is not clearly developed, even granting that it is a joke. The difference between jua (sun) and juha (fool) is not in the initial consonant but in the presence of the medial "h." Furthermore both characters use chua, as does the joke author in the lead, so the difference in pronunciation is not strongly depicted. This is really more of a joke based on a homonym than a joke based upon phonological modification.

if James does not understand miku he can then interpret it as a thing that is with Shem rather than "foot."[1]

Joke 55 depects three types of misunderstandings. Only the second of these involves phonological interference--a complex mispronunication and misinterpretation with the verb -piga.

J55:

Karume alikwenda kwa rafiki yake Mutua akamwambia hivi:
Karume: Mutua nakuomba ukanisatie kazi.
Mutua: Waniomba kwani mimi munguwaka ukitaka kwenda kanisani ukaombe wacha kuniambia ati unaniomba.
Karume: Apana sikukuomba kama watu kanisani yaani nataka ukaniza itie ushikilie namimi nivikilie.
Mutua: Uvikilie nini atamimi apa ninapikilia kwenda ndukani saa tano unusu.
Karume: Apana sikupikilia kwa kili nikupikilia misumali.
Mutua: Kupikilia kiasi kile utanunua nunua kilo tano.
Karume: Wewe uelewi navile ninasama.
Mutua: Wewe unasema nimelewa chupa. Gapi umenipa wewe?
Karume: Kwenda uko ujui kitu wewe.
Muta: Wataka niende kwenu ama uko kwetu ama ni west ama esiti.
Karume: wewe mbure.
Mutua: Na wewe mbure.

Capsule translation--
Karume asks (-omba) his friend Mutua for help. Mutua responds to an alternate meaning of -omba (pray) and tells Karume to go to church. Karume tells Mutua he wants him to hold [nails] while he hits them, "-vikilie" (standard: -pigilie), but Mutua interprets this as "visit" (standard: -fika). Karume tries again but this time says "-pikilia" which Mutua interprets as "cook" (standard -pika). At this point Karume tells Mutua that he doesn't understand, "uelewi" (standard: huelewi), and Mutua interprets this as "to be drunk" (standard: -lewa).

This is a complex joke. The first misunderstanding (involving -omba "to beg for aid, to pray[to God]") is not caused by faulty pronunciation but is rather a problem of two accepted meanings for the same (Standard) form. The second misunderstanding, however, involves a string of related mispronunciations each with different interpretations. In line 6 Karume starts this string by saying

---

[1] Without the phonological alteration of miguu, this joke easily becomes only a pun on the multiple meanings of na.

"to hit [nails]" as -vikilie (standard--with subjunctive suffix -e: -pigilie).[1] Mutua uses the same pronunciation (line 7) but interprets it as "to visit (with)" (standard: -fikilie). Mutua continues speaking (line 7) and produces his own mispronunciation of "think (about)" by saying -pikilia (standard: -fikiria). Karume then uses this same pronunciation, first apparently with Mutua's meaning by saying "I'm not thinking about you" (sikupikilia, line 9) and then trying again to say "hit nails" (standard: -pigilia misumari) by continuing to use this same form -pikilia misumali (line 9) Mutua responds (line 10) by interpreting this as if it were the double prepositional form of "to cook" (standard stem: -pika).[2] Finally, the joke's third misunderstanding occurs as Karume exclaims to Mutua that he "doesn't understand," using the standard form -elewi (line 11). Mutua responds to this as if it were -lewa (be drunk) and asks Karume how many bottles he has brought him (line 12). In terms of the amount of misunderstandings it contains, especially the string of pronunciation and interpretation errors surrounding the intended form -pigilia (hit [nails]), Joke 55 is something of a tour de force among these vichekesho.

Joke 73 involves the mispronunciation of kodi (tax), as does Joke 15. In this joke, however, the modification is different in that here kodi is said as "koti" (coat), the same as the word it it confused with:

J73:

Bwana Onyango katika hekaheka lake la kutafuta pombe
alikutana na jirani wake Omolo mambo yakawa hivi:
Onyango: Jambo omera.

---

[1] All of these mispronunciations are of verb stems with prepositional suffixes, and for -piga the double (intensive) prepositional forms: -piga (to hit), -pigia (to hit with), -pigilia (to pound, ram). It is possible that the comic effect of altering the stem initial consonant is enhanced by the (poetic?) -ilia/e repetition of the endings.

[2] The SS-ED does not list a double prepositional form for -pika, only the prepositional form -pikia. However -pikilia would be the standard for a created double prepositional form.

Omolo: Chambo sana bwala onyango apori yako?
Onyango: Muturi sana jadha, labda, yako?
Omolo: Wewe naweza kojoa pali iko maji ya wasee leo?
Onyango: Iko kwa pwala omar. Lakini pwala omolo wewe nakisa liba koti ya wanaume?
Omolo: Koti gani jadha? Likuwa mimi olikopa koti ya nani?
Onyango: Mimi apala uliza koti ile ya kufaa.
Omolo: Na koti gani tena?
Onyango: Mimi nauliza kama wanakisakata wewe.
Omolo: Sikia sasa omera, kama wewe bado kojoa sawa sawa chungu ya maneno wewe joa kabisa
Onyango: oridi omera.

Capsule translation--[1]
Mr. Omolo is searching for a beerdrink and meets his neighbor Onyango who tells him that beer is at Omar's place. Onyango then asks Omolo if he has paid "koti ya wanaume" [meaning men's tax (but pronouncing koti (coat) instead of the standard kodi)]. Omolo then asks what "koti" is he talking about. When Onyango explains what he meant, Omolo tells him that he doesn't know how to use words.

Onyango tells Omolo where the beer-drink is and tries to see if Omolo has money by asking if he has paid his tax (lines 7-8). The confusion results from Onyango's pronunciation of kodi (tax) as "koti" (coat, line 8). Omolo is confused and says, in effect, "what coat" (koti gani, line 9) and "whose coat" (koti ya nani, lines 9-10). Onyango says that he wasn't speaking of "coat that is worn" (koti ile ya kufaa, line 11). When Omolo asks "Then what coat?" (na koti gani tena?, line 12), Onyango replies that he really wanted to know if Omolo still had money (literally: hadn't been consumed [by taxes], line 13). Omolo tells Onyango that if he doesn't know what he is saying then he is dumb (lines 14-15).

Joke 75 is distinctive as one of the only two jokes among all 133 jokes involving an obvious sexual reference.[2] It is also the

---

[1] In the lead Onyango is identified as the person looking for beer but this is changed in the exchange so that it is Omolo looking for beer and Onyango asking about the tax. Rather than alter the character identifications of the exchange I transposed the names in the lead. (I am assuming that this is just a simple error on the author's part.)

[2] The other joke is not discussed since it does not depict a speech misunderstanding but instead an act of (mistaken?) sodomy.

only joke where a speech misunderstanding is caused by a European mispronouncing a Swahili word.

J75: Bibi na Bwana ambao walikuwa watalii
waliofunza kiswahili kidogo kabla ya
kurejea hapa mjini Nairobi katika
New Stanley Hotel mambo yalikuwa hivi:
Bibi: Weita! (akiinua uma) angalia kuma
yangu kombo kombo namna gani? Taka
ingine. Nini taka wewe!
Weita: (kicheko) Uliza Bwana yako.
Bibi: Darling what did the waiter say.
Bwana: Just shut up!

Capsule translation--
Two European tourists [a man and wife] studied a little Swahili before coming to Nairobi. In a hotel the woman calls to the waiter in poor Swahili to examine her bent fork [uma] but says kuma [vagina] and adds taka wewe [(I) want you]. The waiter responds (laughing) to this sexual offer by saying "ask your husband."

The woman, using what little Swahili she knows, says "kuma" (vagina) instead of uma (fork, line 5). Her entire utterance can be construed as having a sexual reference after this initial mistake (i.e. observe my vagina [it] is crooked . . . [I] want you). The waiter then responds to this interpretation by telling her she must obtain her husband's permission.

Joke 108 depicts three different speech misunderstandings (for which it is nearly the equal of Joke 55)--all of these involving phonological interference:

J108:
Okelo alikuwa akimweleza kamau vile mikatani
iliyochomwa kwa moto ilivyo. Mazungumuzo yakawa hivi:
Okello: Bwana kamau onakojoa bile makonge ile onakwisa
chomwa na mwoto ilivyo?
Kamau: Ala bwana okero hapa tuko nawe unaniona
nikikojoa?
Okello: Osikasirike bwana mimi olikuwa okisema habari
ya makonge tu. Hii makonge ya hapa si kama ya
kwetu nyandha maana ikichomwa na mwoto yeye
osiweze kokuwa tena anakufa tu. Lakini ya hapa
anakuwa tu.
Kamau: Kumbe makonge yanatofautiana? Nirikuwa
nikidhani yote ni dhawa.
Okello: Wololo kata wewe bile bile osiweze kuolewa.
Makonge si dawa.
Kamau: (kwa ghadhabu) Wewe okero sasa unanitusi.

Umekwisha ona mume, aliye ozwa. Mimi nirikuwa nikisema makonge ni aina moja.

Capsule translation--
Okelo was telling Kamau about the sisal leaves which were burning. He says -kojoa for "know" [standard: -jua, infinitive form kujua]. Kamau takes this as the standard form for "urinate" and accuses Okelo of watching him. Okelo denies this, and proceeds to say that the sisal here is different from that in his home, which is dangerous (poisonous) to burn. Kamau says that he thought all sisal was dhawa "same" [standard: sawa]. Okelo interprets this as dawa "medicine" and cautions Kamau not to kuolewa [drink, be drunk; standard: kulewa]. Kamau takes this as the standard form for "to marry [for a woman only]" and thinks it is an insult.

Both of Okelo's mistakes are similar insofar that the phonological modifications that he produces result in other standard forms whose meaning is used by Kamau. Instead of kujua (to know) he says "-kojoa" (to urinate, line 3) and instead of kulewa (drink)[1] he says "kuolewa" (to marry, used only for a woman--the form for a man is kuoa, line 14). Kamau's speech error, on the other hand, does not yield another standard form. He says "dhawa" for sawa (same line 12) but this is then interpreted by Okelo as dawa (medicine).

Joke 94 contains a speech misunderstanding which is caused by the same speech error as in the first misunderstanding in Joke 108:

J94:

Odongo alikwenda kwa mpenzi
wake Cherop, walipokutana walianza
Kusalamiana hivi:
Odongo: Ojambo sana dada
Cherop: Mimi dada yako tena na
ulitaka tuoane?
Odongo: Oh lololo! Okumbe we
bado kojoa kusema nyamuna hiyo
ni kopenda we sana.
Cherop: hadi unataka nikojoe hili
unipende? Sikutaki tena nenda
ukatafute mpenzi atakaekukujolea.

---

[1]In fact, kulewa, even if said properly, would be the wrong since it primarily means "be drunk, intoxicated. Kula (eat) or kunywa (drink) would be appropriate.

Capsule translation--
Odongo greets his girlfriend Cherop using the term dada [sister]. She asks how she can be his sister and marry him. When Odongo tries to explain that it is term of endearment he says "kojoa" instead of kujua [to know]. Cherop takes this as the standard form for "urinate" and tells Odongo that she doesn't want him and to find some girl who will urinate for/on him.

There are two misunderstandings in this joke. The first does not involve an error in pronunciation but rather multiple meanings of dada (sister, girlfriend). The second misunderstanding is the result of phonological interference --kujua (to know) pronounced as "kojoa" (to urinate) by Odongo in line 8. Cherop accepts the standard form kojoa as an improper (and obscene) suggestion by Odongo.

The last entry in this group of jokes concerning phonological-based speech misunderstandings is Joke 129. It involves a radical phonological modification and a misunderstanding which is not clear:

J129:

Siku moja Njuguna alitamani kula mkate ya chapati hivyo alitoka akaenda dukani kwa Mhindi kununua Unga mweupe wa Ngano. Ingali aje hakufahamu lugha ya taifa barabara alifika dukani mwa Shah Provision Store na maongezi yao ya kawa hivi:

Njuguna: Muindi, nataka mutuangano.
Mhindi: Alitaka nini?
Njuguna: Nataka Mutuangano.
Mhindi: [(]Alienda huko nyuma la duka akatoa kabuti harafu akarejea huku akikunja mikono la sharti ili ampokee Njuguna Mutuangano. Njuguna kuona vile alitimua mbio huku akisema, Muindi usinifike, hapana teka bala mimi. Sasa watu wengine hapo kati ya wale wanunusi walimwambia Mhindi kuwa yeye huyo Njuguna alitaka unga wa Ngano Wale Siyo Kutuanganana. Haraka Mhindi alielewa kuwa Kiswahili chao ndicho kilikongana, hivyo tena ikawa namna hii.[(]
Mhindi: Bai, mambia ile matu rundi nunua iko Unga Ngano tele. Sasa Vite hapana.
Njuguna: [(]haye kule alikate mitaa moja kwa moja hadi nyumbani. Sijui kama Unga alirundi kununua ama alinunua kesho yake.[)]

Capsule translation--
Njuguna goes into an Indian's shop to buy wheat flour "Unga . . . Ngano." He does not understand the language of the streets. In the shop he asks for "mutuangano." The Indian asks him what is it that he wants and he

> repeats it. So the Indian goes to the back and gets an overcoat [kabuti] and folds the sleeves so that he can give it to Njunga as a mutuangano. [It isn't clear what the Indian thinks this is; nor is it clear why, when seeing it--] Njuguna flees the shop. Other customers tell the Indian that Njuguna really wanted "unga wa ngano" [wheat flour] but Njuguna has run home.

The misunderstanding of the joke is not clear, but it is readily apparent that Njuguna's use of the pronunciation of "mutuangano" (lines 6, 8) (instead of unga wa ngano) causes the Indian shopkeeper to produce an overcoat in such a way (sleeves folded) that Njuguna is startled and runs home.

The following group of jokes involve misunderstandings that are based upon grammatical variations of Standard Swahili.

In Joke 7 a patient answers his doctor's questions with nonsense due to grammatical errors:

J7:
Bwana Otugo alikwenda hospitali kutaka kutibiwa, na Daktari alipokuwa akimhoji, Otugo alimweleza ugonjwa wake.
Daktari: Jina lako nani?
Otugo: Jina lake Otugo.
Daktari: Unaumwa wapi?
Otugo: Tumbo nauma, kichwa nahara damu, muguu natemekatemeka awesi kwenda.
Daktari: Ugonjwa huu ulikuanza limi?
Otugo: Aliwanza keso bwana.

Capsule translation--
Otugo goes to the hospital and tells the doctor, in grammatically confused Swahili, that his stomach is hurting, his head has diarrhea, and he got sick tomorrow.

In response to the doctor's first question, Otugo uses the wrong possessive pronoun form and instead of saying "My name is Otugo" (Jina langu Otugo) he says, "Jina lake Otugo" (His name is Otugo, line 4). When asked where the pain is, Otugo mixes his nouns and says that his head (instead of his stomach/intestine) has bloody diarrhea, for "kichwa [head] nahara damu [passes blood]" (line 6). His final mistake is not grammatical, but is rather a mistake in lexical choice as he states (line 9) that his illness started "keso" (tomorrow; standard: kesho).

Joke 14 depicts a misunderstanding caused by a European manager's use of a grammatically attenuated and incorrect verb phrase:

J14:

Hapa ni Shamba la Mkonge. Siku moja Mtu mmoja alikuja kutafuta Kazi ya kukata Mkonge. Na Kumbuka ya kuaamba hapa ukishandikiwa kazi ya kukata Mkonge. Unapewa kisu na ifikapo Mwisho wa mwezi. Unakatwa pesa ya Kisu kwa msahara yako. MAMBO YAKAWA HIVI:

Ongaro: Bwana mimi nataka kazi ya kukata Mkonge.
Mzungu: Unajua kazi ya kukata mkonge?
Ongaro: Ndio nimekwisha kata huko MWATATE SISAL ESTATE.
Mzungu: Haya basi hiko kazi, sasa kwenda sitoo ukate kisu huko.
Ongaro: Mimi sijui kukata kisu, najua kukata mkonge tu. Kisu naweza kukata kisu namna gani" Mimi bado Kuona kazi hiyo.
Mzungu: Hapana mimi nasema kwenda kwa sitoo, huko utapata Karani atapewa wewe kisu, lakini pesa yako atakata siku ya msahara yako unasikia?
Ongaro: Hala kumbe namna hiyo, hiyo mzuri tu, H[N]asikia sasa maneno.

Capsule Translation--
Ongaro applies for work cutting sisal. He is told by the European manager, in grammatically confused Swahili, to go to the clerk and "ukate kisu" [European means: he will get a knife and have its cost cut from his salary]. Ongaro thinks he is supposed to cut "kisu" [knife] and tells the manager he doesn't know how to do this. The manager explains what he meant and Ongaro agrees.

In the lead, there is an explanation of the process by which a new employee is issued a knife for cutting sisal and its cost taken at the end of the month unakatwa pesa ya kisu kwa msahara [standard: mshahara] yako (literally: you are cut the money of the knife from your wage, lines 4-5). In the exchange, however, the European manager tells Ongaro to go to the [company] store ("sitoo") and "ukate kisu" (literally: You should cut a knife, lines 9-10). The manager has produced a verb phrase in which kisu (knife) is the direct object of -kate (should cut). Ongaro interprets the manager's words as they are given and states that he doesn't know how to "cut a knife, only sisal" (line 11). The manager then corrects himself and explains what he means in the more standard "pesa yako atakata" (your money he [clerk, "kanani"] will cut).

Joke 21 depicts a European's "broken" Swahili (often called Kisettla, meaning the Swahili variety used by the European settlers) as responsible for the use of his cat for the evening meal:

J21:

Kulikua na Mzungu na bibi wake na mfanyi kazi[.] siku moja bibi wa Mzungu alisafiri akabaki mfanyikazi na Mzungu wa kiume. Mzungu akamuita mfanyikazi Jon.

[Mzungu:] kuya haba.
Jon: haya nimekuja bwana.
Mzungu: leo utapika nini kwamimi wee jua pikapika.
Jon: nitajaribu.
Mzungu: leo pika kukupaka.
Jon: haya bwana.

[(]Mzungu alikua, ana fuga paka lake kuwa kibande cha pusi. Mzungu akaenda zake kazini, Jon akaanza kufukuza lile pande la paka maramoja akalishika akalichinja na kupika vitu vyote vikawa tayali saa 5 Mzungu kaingia akaketi kungojea saa 6 ifike ndipo ale. Mzungu anatupa macho huku na huku paka halioni kilasiku akiingia hulikuta mlangoni, saa imefika akawekewa chakula mezani kuziona akagutu lakini akasema nitauliza bada ya kushiba. Tayali ameshiba anatafuta paka wake ampe nyama akaita Jon nam.[)]

Mzungu: Paka yangu yuwapi.
Jon: [(]akajibu[)] si hiyo unakula.
Mzungu: nani na chinja.
Jon: mimi.
Bwana[Mzungu]: mimi nakula paka yangu maigodi mmmmmm majiga wewe pika paka yangu mimi kula mamsapu kuya hapa piga gumi moja wewe ona nywele yangu naanza toka moyamoya kama majani ya miti gozi nawekawapi mimi taka tengeneza kofia ya pusi yangu na wewe kazi hakuna kwenda jako kama chelewa chelewa wewe pata gumi moja ya mamsapu.

[(]Jona akatoka na kukimbia mbio.[)]

Capsule translation--
European's wife leaves for a trip leaving him with their cook, Jon. European tells Jon, in grammatically confusing Swahili, to cook something for him and to cook chicken for his cat. Jon cooks the cat for supper and the European eats it and becomes enraged when he asks where the cat is and learns he has eaten it.

The European intends to tell Jon to cook some chicken for the cat, but his Swahili is shorn of grammatical devices. He says "pika kukupaka" (literally: cook chicken cat, line 10). (A standard arrangement, with the necessary verb affixes and particles, would be umpikie kuku kwa paka.) The cook interprets the European's actual request as meaning that he should cook the cat--which he does. The remainder of the joke depicts the European's startling discovery that he has eaten his cat.

In Joke 33, a policeman produces a sentence with the verb object and the dependent clause object exchanged.

J33:

Askari polisi alimshika Sudi akiendesha baiskeli bila taa:
Askari: Ewe Kijana, we napanda taa hakuna baskili.
Sudi: Mzee, nitapandaje taa bila baiskeli.
Askari: Sikia mitoto, wewe osilete miswahili yako.
Sudi: Hewallah afande, sasa hebu nijaribu kuipanda taa hii ya chemni niliyotoka kuinunua nawe nikuachie baiskeli.
Askari: Wewe ndiye mwenye makosa. Sisi takamata wewe.
Sudi: Vipi bwana askari, mimi ninayo taa, baiskeli ndiyo haina.
Askari: Wewe ndiyo naendesa baskili.
Sudi: Mimi sikuilazimisha ila yenyewe ndiyo iliyokubali Kunibeba.
Askari: Wewe mitoto ilo sida kubwa haya kwenda.

Capsule translation--
Sudi is stopped for riding a bicycle without a light but the policeman mixes up his words and says you are riding a light without a bicycle ["taa bila baskili"]. Sudi says that this isn't possible and the policeman replies don't [confuse matters with your Swahili]. Sudi then tries to talk his way out by saying that he will ride the chimney lantern he has just bought and the policeman can take the bicycle. The policeman says I'll arrest you. Sudi then says that he has a lantern but it is the bicycle which doesn't. The policeman says but you were riding it. Sudi says he only hitched a ride. The policeman says you are too much trouble, go away.

A policeman (askari polisi) stops Sudi who is riding a bicycle without a headlight (taa). However, by mixing his word order, the policeman asks Sudi why he is "napanda taa hukuna baskili"--which literally means "riding a light without a bicycle" (line 2). The grammatical arrangement (although still not standard due to the use of hakuna "there is not" for "without" instead of bila) should have been -panda baskili . . . taa. Sudi exclaims that this--i.e. riding a light without a bicycle--is not possible. (The rest of the exchange is essentially grammatical.)

Jokes 63 and 84 both depict the same grammatical error, an incorrect interrogative sentence, which allows the other character to create a pun:

J63:

Mchana moja kikana alikua na motoka yake
akiwa anaendesha mbio sana na motoka yake
haikuako na taa yambele alipo ona polisi
Barabarani akisimamisha motoka yake ilikua
ina kwenda mbio tuu alikua angali anasukuma
chuma tuu na motoka ilikua haina breki tena
na mambo yakawa hivi:
Polisi: Wewe, wapi taa? (kijana)
Kijana: Ndiyo naapitaa.
Polisi: [(]Kwa Haraka Polisi auliza [)]wapi taa?
Kijana: [(]Kijana Huku anaendesha motoka yake mbio Kijana [)]ndiyo na pitaa.
Polisi: [(]Akauliza[)]motoka yako lakini haina breki? "Kwanini unapeleka motoka yake mbio namna hii?
Kijana: [(]Akajibu Kwa Haraka[)]breki nimemuacha nyumbani wakila meirungi na Abedi.
Kwa uerevu kija kajiepusha akapita Hakushikwa.

Capsule translation--
One day a youth was driving a car without lights or brakes. He is hailed by a policeman who ungrammatically asks "wapi taa?" [where lights]. The youth interprets this as the verb wapita [you are passing] and yells back "napitaa" [I am passing]. The rest of the joke is not clear--but not seemingly ungrammatical. Asked about his "breki" (brakes) the youth says he left them home.)

J84:

Usiku mmoja mwendesha baiskeli isiyokuwa na taa
alikutana na askari (polisi) mambo yakawa hivi:
Askari: Hee!! Hee!! Wapi Taa.
Mwendesha (Baiki) Baiskeli: Na Pitaa.
Askari: Simama.
Mwendesha Baiskeli: Sina Baba wala Mama.

Capsule translation--
One night a rider of a bicycle without lights met a policeman. The policeman says "wapi taa" [where lights] and the rider responds as if this was the verb form wapita and says "napitaa" [I am passing]. The policeman says "simama" [halt] and the rider responds as if this were the negative si [is not] and mama [mother] by saying "sina Baba wala mama"[I do not have a father or mother].

Both jokes involve a play upon the grammatically incorrect interrogative form wapi taa (standard: taa iko wapi). But this incorrect form is then somewhat similar to the verb form wapita (you are passing)[1] (except that the stress and intonation would be different) and can be cleverly answered with napita (I am passing). Joke 84 also includes the additional word play upon simama, but this is not based upon a grammatical error as simama is the standard imperative form.

The last joke of this group of grammatically-based misunderstandings is Joke 113. This joke involves a confusion over the object of the verb "to eat," due in part to the ommission of a locative suffix on the place noun following the verb:

J113:

Bwana John alikuwa anatembea
Katika soko moja wakati wa mchana ndipo
alikutana na rafikiye na mambo
yakawa hivi:
John: Hujambo bwana Daudi?
Daudi: Sijambo nipatie shilingi
moja nikule naye hoteli.
John: Hoteli iko wapi?
Daudi: Hoteli iko kule Karibu na
duka ya mwisho (wakaelekea
hotelini) ndio hil bwana.
John: utawezaje kula nyumba!
Daudi: hapana nyumba! ni Vya-
Kula vilivio ndani ya
hoteli.

Capsule translation--
John is walking in the market at noon when he meets his friend Daudi. Daudi asks him for a shilling so that he can eat "naye hoteli" [with you (at) the hotel]. John, apparently not knowing what hoteli means asks where it is. When Daudi shows him he exclaims "are you going to eat the building!"

Hoteli (derived from the English "hotel"), as a noun, should have a locative particle or suffix when it is referred to as a place. Here, however, Daudi does not use any locative device (e.g. hotelini, with the locative suffix -ni), and therefore nikule naye hoteli (line 7) is interpreted as "eat with you a hoteli."

---

[1]The standard form of the verb would be -pita not -pitaa. The additional -a can be seen as a represention of a shout (or emphasis) and/or as a device for pointing out the similarity to taa (light).

[It should be noted, however, that this is not a standard phrase (standard: nile nawe) but it is not clear whether this deviation is grammatical or due to phonological interference.]

Absence of Stereotypes Concerning Speech Misunderstandings Based Upon IMV Swahili

The manner in which phonologically and grammatically variant Swahili is depicted as a cause of speech misunderstandings in these jokes does not permit a strong conclusion concerning the presence of beliefs about its communicational efficiency. The area in which the strongest conclusion can be made is in the relationship between interlocutor familiarity and the joke setting. At the beginning of this section it was assumed that variation in speech form should be a source of misunderstanding between interlocutors who are not (very) familiar with each other's speech. This assumption is supported by the joke situations. In eleven of the sixteen jokes, the characters are probably strangers: Policeman-citizen--J1, J33, J63, J84; customer-clerk--J75, J129; patient-doctor--J7; manager-(new) employee--J14; fellow workers (but who are not characterized as friends)--J108; and characters met in the street--J32,[1] J36. Four of the five exceptions depict two rafiki (friends)--J55, J73, J94, J113. The other exception, J21, depicts a (European) employer and his cook; however, it might be argued that this is not really an exception since the joke's lead suggests that the employer does not speak with his cook often and does so now only because his wife is gone.

It is also significant that in all but three of the jokes the exchanges are located in public settings. The street is the most common, used in six of the eleven exchanges in which the characters are not familiar to each other--J15, J32, J36, J33, J84; and even in two jokes in which the characters are friends--J73, J113. The other

[1]In Joke 32 Oiro and Fred are not characterized by any relationship. Their meeting place is not specified, but can be assumed to be on a street as Oiro has just bought sun glasses. An additional feature of characterization which suggests a probable lack of familiarity is the difference in names--Oiro is a "tribal" name and Fred is a Western/Christian name.

public settings are a restaurant--J75; a business or work-place--J108, J129, J14; and a hospital--J7. The other three exchanges are all located in a home, all where the characters are familiar to each other--J55,[1] J94, and J21. The fact that there are many public settings, while not conclusive by itself, at least suggests that these conversations are probably not representations of informal--even intimate--speech events among familiar interlocutors.

At this point a tentative conclusion can be drawn concerning the communicational efficiency of spoken, interference-marked Swahili in Kenya. Based upon this discussion of the kinds of interlocutors, and settings, depicted in these jokes, it seems apparent that one consistent theme of these jokes is that of strangers using IMV Swahili in public places and being misunderstood. The presence of this theme is (at least) consistent with the existence of a stereotypic belief that spoken, IMV, Swahili is not an efficient medium of national communication. However, this conclusion is greatly tempered by an examination of the predictability of the speech and the topics which are misunderstood.

If, as was discussed at the beginning of this section, the predictability of a speech form is related inversely to the possibility that it will be misunderstood if it is mispronounced, then only a few of the exchanges depicted in these jokes should have resulted in a misunderstanding (J55, J108, and, possibly, J73). In each joke situation the message which was intended by one of the characters should reasonably have been expected by the other and understood in spite of the variation in speech form. For example, the policeman in Joke 15 could have been expected to be asking for a kodi (tax receipt) as an identification for someone walking at night when he says kothi--not a koti (coat). Similarly, in Jokes 63 and 84, a policeman hailing a cyclist without lights is more likely to mean "where is your light" than "you are passing" when he ungrammatically says wapi taa. Even the few exchanges where the

---

[1]In Joke 55 there is no explicit setting given, but in the lead one character "goes to" (alikwenda kwa, line 1) his friend, and I think it is reasonable to assume that this is a home.

message does not appear to be completely expected are not really unpredictable. In Joke 55, Karume's request for help in pounding nails is not necessarily expected since he is not identified as a carpenter; but even so this is a request for help with an ordinary task in contemporary Kenya, and could easily be anticipated.

These jokes do not, therefore, depict spoken, varietal Swahili causing misunderstandings in messages containing new, or unpredictable, information. Related to this point is the absence of any messages, predictable, or not, concerning national affairs. There are no speech misunderstandings in which varietal Swahili fails to convey a message concerning economics, labor unions, government organization, or court procedure, to name only a few areas of Kenyan national affairs.

The results of the analyses in this section are equivocal. On the basis of depicted interlocutors there is some support for concluding that there is a belief, manifested in the jokes, about the communicational inefficiency of spoken Swahili. However, this conclusion cannot be strongly stated in terms of national utility since spoken Swahili is not at the same time clearly depicted as failing to convey messages relating to nationalistic development of Kenya.

Speech Misunderstandings Based Upon English Loans and the Use of English

Swahili speakers in Kenya, have in varying degrees, lived within a social and political milieu dominated by English speakers. English has played an extremely important role in a country that is becoming increasingly modernized along Western (English) models. In these circumstances, English loans, and the use of English words or phrases, should show up in Swahili speech, and therefore constitute a potential source of confusion which would be depicted in the jokes.

Even a casual examination of a small number of joke exchanges reveals that English words, and phrases, are commonly employed in speech depiction. For example, each of the first four jokes in the Appendix contains at least one English form. Briefly, without giving each joke in full, in Joke 1, line 4, there is "Africa" and in line 12 the initials "U.K." which actually stand for United Kisumu but which is supposed to be an admiring copy of the same initials for United Kingdom. In Joke 2 the speech of one character (albeit a European) is entirely in English. In Joke 3, lines 1, 9 and 11, there is the English-based loan stima (from "steam") meaning electricity. In Joke 4 there is the personal name Peter for one of the characters. Interestingly, only in Joke 2 does the use of English create misunderstanding. Here the other character, a beginning student who does not know English, attempts to decode English words as if they were Swahili.

This last example, in fact, can serve as a model for many of the jokes in which the presence of English creates confusion. For this reason it will be given in full:

J2:

Mtoto mwanafunzi alienda Shuleni Siku
yake ya kwanza na Wakakutana na Mzungu, na vile
Mtoto hakuelewa Kisungu Vizuri Mambo yalikua
hivi:
Mzungu: Good Morning boy!
Mtoto: Mimi si boi yako ya kukupikia
chakula jikoni!
Mzungu: How are you?
Mtoto: At ari yuu ndio Kusema nini?
Mzungu: Say fine Sir'
Mtoto: At faini ya Saa?
Basi Mtoto vile hakuelewa kizungu Kusikia
fine Sir akafikiria Mzunga amesema
atoe faini ya Saa alitimua mbio
Kama Suara mpaka nyumbani
hakurudi tena Shuleni Mpaka Sasa.

A student who is a child (mtoto) and who does not know English mistakes the English of a European (mzungu) teacher for similar sounding Swahili words. On his first day at school, the child is greeted by the European in English (iine 5) but the child interprets the English "boy" as the Swahili form boi (originally an English loan) which means a servant in a derogatory sense (i.e. houseboy). The child responds, "Mimi si boi yako ya kukupikia chakula jikoni" (I am not your boy for cooking food in the kitchen, lines 6-7). A second misunderstanding occurs when the European tells him to say "fine Sir." The child thinks "fine" is the Swahili faini (an English loan meaning a punishment/penalty) and "Sir" [pronounced as the British "sah"] is the Swahili saa (clock, hour). The child thinks he will be punished and so runs home and does not return.

One other example will be given to illustrate this kind of misunderstanding. In this joke, however, it is an isolated English word--menu--which is misunderstood:

J31:

Kichekesho kikubwa kilitokea majuzi wakati Songoro alipokuwa katika nyendo zake mitaani na kwa ghafla akakutana na Kisura mmoja alie kuwa nadhifu mwenye Pochi kubwa, wigi, na stoking. Baadae walielewana lugha hivyo Songoro akampeleka Hoteli ili wapate Chakula.

Songoro: Waonaje bibie?
Kipusa: Sijambo bwana.
Songoro: Naona kama nakuelewa, nadhani tulikutana zamani.
Kipusa: Pengine labda, wajua mambo ni ....
Songoro: Haidhuru utamalizia Hoteli, hebu twende tukapate mlo.

Songoro: Weita? Hebu tafdhali niletee Menu. Je bibi utakula nini?
Kipusa: Hata mimi nitakula hio hio menu.
Songoro: Samahani bibi, menu sio chakula bali ni orodha ya vyakula.

Songoro meets a young lady and after chatting for a while they go to a *hoteli* (tea stall/cafe) for something to eat (line 1-11). At the cafe Songoro tells the waiter to bring him a menu (*niletee* Menu," line 12) and asks the girl what she would like ("*utakula nini?*" lines 12-13). She says she will eat the same thing--a menu ("*nitakula hio hio* menu," line 14). Songoro corrects her by telling her that a menu is not food (*chakula*) but a listing of foods ("*orodha ya vyakula*," lines 15-16). This joke is different from Joke 2 in that the English word is not reinterpreted as another, similar Swahili form, but rather simply accepted as an unknown word whose meaning is then guessed. In either case, the presence of the strange, English forms created a misunderstanding.

Depictions like these in the jokes would seem to lend support to a conclusion that the presence and use of English is really a barrier to communication because it produces another group of strange and unknown speech forms in an already heterogeneous linguistic situation. However, for as many jokes as there are of this kind, there are as many, if not more, in which English forms are used and not misunderstood. In one joke, for example, an English-based form (betri, "battery") is used to clarify a problem involving a Swahili homonym (Joke 12, see above, page 46).

English is a foreign language, and the majority of Kenyans are not familiar with it, however, it does function as a lingua franca of national communication, particularly among the educated and the elite. Although English is not clearly depicted as a source of speech misunderstanding in these jokes it could be considered as an elitist language and correspondingly depicted as communicting only restricted, Western/technical meanings.

This assumption is not supported by joke content. English is used for such ordinary objects as coffee (Joke 10), menus Jokes 31 and 111), and straws (Joke 59), and is misunderstood. It is also used for "Industrial Area" (Joke 45), "office" (Joke 11), and battery (betri, Joke 12), and is understood. There is, moreover, no no restricted use of English for technical and scientific domains and so in this regard there does not appear to be any prestige differential beteen English and Swahili in the jokes.

There is one aspect of the way in which English-based misunderstandings are depicted which could support a conclusion that it is considered to be a prestige language. This involves misinterpretations relative to Swahili.

The creation of homonyms across language is not an unexpected or unusual process.[1] It is essentially the same process of decoding described in the preceding section by which a form in varietal Swahili is decoded as a different form in Standard Swahili. What is noteworthy is the direction in which this process operates in these jokes. In no joke is there a Swahili form decoded as an English form, either by an African or a European character. (The

---

[1]Mary Haas describes something very much like this process in her two articles, "Thai Word Games" and "Interlingual Word Taboo." In the first, she describes a children's game which involves moving from Thai words to phonetically similar English words. In the second, she describes the restrictions ("taboos") placed upon the use of certain Thai words because they are phonetically similar to obscene English words.

vernaculars need not be considered as a possible comparison since they do not appear to any great extent in the jokes and when they do appear, e.g. Joke 51, they are not interpreted as anything else). There is only one joke in which one English form is mistaken for another. Joke 122 depicts a misunderstanding involving the confusion of one English word for another English word.

J122:

Mr. Wakimwere na mzungu wake. mzungu
alikuwa akiita Wakimwere "fool" wakati wote,
siku moja walikwenda town. Mzungu akamuliza
Wakimwere kama angetaka kununua tikiti ya
Kenya Pools.
Wakimwere [(]akaduwaa kidogo na akajibu[):] ndio.
Mzungu [(] aka mwambia [):] lete pesa.
Wakimwere [(]akauliza mzungu[):] hata wewe utanunua.
Mzungu [(] akajibu[):] ndio.
Wakimwere[(]akamwambia mzungu[):] Kumbe hata wewe ni fool.
Mzungu[:] kwa nini?
Wakimwere [(]akasema[):] kwa sababu unanunua tikiti ya "fool."
Mzungu akanyamaza na akagoma kuita wakimwene fool.

A European (*mzungu*) is constantly calling his servant Wakimwere a "fool" (lines 1-2). One day they go to town and the European asks Wakimwere if he is going to buy a ticket (*tikiti*) from the Kenya Pools [a state-run lottery] (lines 3-5). Wakimwere says yes (*ndio*) and then asks the European if he is going to buy a ticket. The European says yes and Wakimwere says "Why then you are a fool" (*kumba hata wewe ni* fool, line 10). When the European asks why, Wakimwere says because you are buying '*tikiti ya* "fool".' (line 12). Apparently the character Wakimwere interprets "pool" as "fool."

There are, however, several jokes in which English is produced in a variant manner, but not misunderstood--in none of these is the varietal English misinterpreted as any other form than English. One example will demonstrate this kind of joke. Joke 107 depicts a situation in which varietal English is used as the point of the joke although not because it is misinterpreted:

J107:

Mazumgumzo juu yaa mshahara kati ya mzungu mwanamke
na mkubwa wa washeremala Bw. Lusima, Mzungu ni "madame"

ndiye Lusima aliambia Madame kwa kiingereza ati washeremala wanataka mshahara wao siku hiyo. Ndiye ikaanza hivi:
Lusima: Oh! mzungu sir
Madam: Yes, Lusima what is the matter?
Lusima: Sir, today peoples want moneys.
Madam: Moneys?
Lusima: Yes moneys, moneys salarying today
Madame: Lusima, Okay you will get money today.
Lusima: Yes, yes sir you are good, gooder, goodest.

Lusima, the foreman of the carpenters (*mkubwa wa washeremala*), has come to the European (*mzungu*) woman employer to ask for their wages (*mshahara*) (lines 1-4). His English is marked by the use of "sir" for a woman, the addition of a plural suffix to "money" and "people," the formation of "salary" as a verb with an "-ing" suffix, and saying "good, gooder, goodest." His English is, however, understood by the woman. It may be that there is an indication in the jokes of a prestige differential between Swahili and English. In essence, this is a manifestation of the belief that Swahili is not dominant and that there is no concern in the jokes about translating something said in Swahili into English whereas, as I have shown at the beginning of this section, there is a concern about the translation of English into Swahili.

Conclusions

Examining the manner in which these jokes depict misunderstandings based upon speech forms and semantic ambiguity yields two conclusions regarding the position of Swahili in popular stereotypes. First, Swahili technical terms do not constitute a basis for joke misunderstandings. Even though misunderstandings that are based upon semantic elaboration are depicted (e.g. in Joke 12, the term *makaa* meaning both "batteries" and "charcoal")--and there can be little doubt that the inevitable semantic elaboration which must accompany modernization is manifested in these jokes--technical, Western scientific elaborations are not depicted as the cause of speech misunderstandings. Consequently, Swahili does not have a popular stereotype as a language which is hampered by technical semantic overloading. Swahili may, in fact, acquire such an unproductive stereotype if its on-going, and future, semantic development into the technical domains now expressed in English is not carefully planned to avoid the type of overleading described by Whiteley (1969). But at the time of this study, no such stereotype is apparent in these jokes.

Second, those misunderstandings that are based upon interference-marked variation in Swahili speech are not depicted as occurring in situations for which Swahili should function as a medium of national communication--i.e. the transmission of information of national interest among "Kenyans," different citizens who are not friends or relatives. This conclusion, however, is somewhat tempered by the fact that most of the misunderstandings are depicted between character types who are probably strangers. Yet these misunderstandings concern such ordinary, predictable speech content that no misunderstanding should have taken place--even with the variation in the characters' speech. Consequently, the conclusion is that there is no consistent expression of a stereotype concerning a deleterious effect of interference-marked variation in the use of spoken Swahili for effective national communication.

Although two conclusions can be reached about what is <u>not</u> present in popular stereotypes, one important questions remains concerning the overall depiction of speech communication in the jokes. Although the specific manner in which Swahili is depicted in the jokes does not indicate the presence of stereotypes abouts is inefficiency as a medium of national communication, it does appear that speech communication in general is stereotyped as an uncertain process involving ambiguity and misunderstanding.

Close to one third of these jokes (44 of 133 jokes) depict an occurrence of a speech misunderstanding of one kind or another. Some of these are based upon changes in the meanings of Swahili words, others are based upon alterations in the form of Swahili speech. Yet almost 40 percent of the misunderstandings are not based upon Swahili but upon misinterpretations of the form and meaning of English words. (In addition there are a few jokes involving the use of vernacular--e.g. Joke 26). Therefore, regardless of their exact causes, the presence of a large number of speech misunderstandings in these jokes suggests the existence of a popular stereotype about the general difficulties of speech communication in Kenya. This kind of stereotypic expression is consistent with the facts of Kenya's linguistic diversity discussed at the beginning of this study: The diversity in the forms of speech due to the different vernaculars and vernacular interference in second languages, and the diversity in speech use and content due to the relatively rapid processes of modernization and Westernization are matters of concern to Kenyans--especially insofar as they must communicate effectively with other Kenyans of different language backgrounds.

BIBLIOGRAPHY

Ainslie, Rosalyne.
1966 The Press in Africa. New York: Walker and Co.

Area Handbook for Kenya
1967 Washington, D. C.: U.S. Government Printing Office (DA PAM No. 550-56).

Berry, Jack, and Joseph Greenberg
1966 Sociolinguistic Research in Africa. African Studies Bulletin (Stanford) 9(2):1-9.

DeLany, Milan G. P.
1967 A Phonological Contrastive Analysis, North American English-Standard Swahili. Swahili 37 (1):27-46.

Doob, Leonard
1961 Communication in Africa: A Search for Boundaries. New Haven: Yale University Press.

Edmonson, Munro
1952 Los Manitos: Patterns of Humor in Relation to Cultural Values. Unpublished Ph.D. Thesis, Harvard University.

Epstein, A. L.
1969 Linguistic Innovation and Culture on the Copperbelt, Northern Rhodesia. Southwestern Journal of Anthropology 15:235-253.

Ferguson, Charles
1959 Diglossia. Word 15:325-340.

Feuereisen, Fritz, and Ernst Schmacke (Compilers)
1969 Africa: A Guide to Newspapers and Magazines. New York: Africana Publishing Co.

Fishman, Joshua
1968a Sociolinguistics and the Language Problems of Developing Countries. In Language Problems of Developing Nations. Fishman, Ferguson and Das Gupta, Eds. New York: Wiley.

1968b Nationality-Nationalism and Nation-Nationism. In Language Problems of Developing Nations. Fishman, Ferguson, and Das Gupta, Eds. New York: Wiley.

1972 Language and Nationalism. Rowley, Massachusetts: Newbury House.

Goldklang, Harold A. (Compiler)
1967 Current Swahili Newspaper Terminology. Swahili 37 (2):194-208.

1968 Current Swahili Newspaper Terminology (Part II Swahili-English). Swahili 38(1):42-53.

Gorman, Thomas

1971a A Survey of Educational Language Policy; and an Inquiry into Patterns of Language Use and Levels of Language Attainment among Secondary School Entrants in Kenya. Unpublished Doctoral dissertation, University of Nairobi.

1971b Sociolinguistic Implications of a Choice of Media of Instruction. In Language Use and Social Change. W. Whiteley, Ed. London: Oxford University Press.

Greenberg, Joseph

1966 The Languages of Africa. Bloomington, Ind.: Indiana University Press.

Gulliver, P. H.

1969 Introduction. In Tradition and Transition in East Africa. P. H. Gulliver, Ed. Berkeley: University of California Press.

Haas, Mary

1951 Interlingual Word Taboos. American Anthropologist 53:338-344.

1957 Thai Word Games. Journal of American Folklore 70: 173-175.

Harries, Lyndon

1968 Swahili in Modern East Africa. In Language Problems of Developing Nations. J. Fishman, C. Ferguson, and J. Das Gupta, Eds. New York: Wiley

Haugen, Einar

1966 Language, Dialect, Nation. American Anthropologist 68:922-930.

Hoenigswald, Henry

1966 A Proposal for the Study of Folk-linguistics. In Sociolinguistics. W. Bright, Ed. The Hague: Mouton.

Hymes, Dell

1962 The Ethnography of Speaking. In Anthropology and Human Behavior. T. Gladwin and W. C. Sturtevant, Eds. Washington, D. C.: Anthropological Society of Washington.

Institute of Swahili Research

1966 Tentative List of New Words, Part I. Swahili 36 (2):169-184.

1967a Tentative List of New Words, Part II. Swahili 37 (1):103-123.

1967b Second Tentative Word List, Part I. Swahili 37 (2):209-244.

1968a Second Tentative Word List, Part II. Swahili 38 (1):54-99.

1968b Second Tentative Word List, Part III. Swahili 38 (2):164-168.

J.W.
n.d. Kisettla. Mimeographed. Nairobi.

Kenya Government
1969 Kenya Population Census. Vols. I-III. Nairobi: Kenya Government Printer.

Kimani, S. R.
1971 Problems in Swahili Use and Phonology, Kiswahili 41 (1):94-99.

Kitcher, Helen, Ed.
1956 The Press in Africa. Washington, D. C.: Ruth Slone Associates.

Koestler, Arthur
1964 The Act of Creation. New York: Dell, Laurel Edition.

Lienhardt, Peter
1968 Introduction. In The Medicine Man: Swifa Ya Nguvumali. Hasani bin Ismail (Peter Linehardt, Editor and Translator). London: Oxford University Press.

Mazrui, Ali A.
1966 The English Language and Political Consciousness in British Colonial Africa. Journal of Modern African Studies 4(3):295-311.

1967 The National Language Question in East Africa. East Africa Journal, June 1967:12-19.

Neale, Barbara
1972 Kenya's Asian Languages. In Language in Kenya Wilfred Whiteley, Ed. London: Oxford University Press.

Nida, Eugene, and William Wonderly
1971 Communication Role of Languages in Multilingual Societies. In Language Use and Social Change. Wilfred Whiteley, Ed. London: Oxford University Press.

Oliver, Roland, and J. D. Fage
1962 A Short History of Africa. Baltimore, Maryland: Penguin Books.

Parkin, David J.
1972 Language Switching in Nairobi. In Language in Kenya. Wilfred Whiteley, Ed. London: Oxford University Press.

Polome, Edgar
1967 Swahili Language Handbook. Washington, D. C.: Center for Applied Linguistics.

Powdermake, Hortense
1962 Copper Town: Changing Africa. New York: Harper and Row.

Rhoades, John
1967 Language Use in Joke Characterizations: A Study of Language Stereotypes in Kenya. Unpublished Ph.D. Dissertation, Syracuse University.

Standard Swahili-English Dictionary.
1939 1st Edition, Reprinted 1967.

Welime, J. D. Wanjala
1970 Some Problems of Teaching Swahili at Advanced Level Kenya. In Language in Education in Eastern Africa. Thomas Gorman, Ed. Nairobi: Oxford University Press.

Whiteley, Wilfred
1968 Ideal and Reality in National Language Policy: Tanzania. In Language Problems of Developing Nations. J. Fishman, C. Ferguson, and J. Das Gupta, Eds. New York: Wiley.

1969 Swahili: The Rise of a National Language. London: Methuen and Company.

1971 Some Factors Influencing Language Policies in Eastern Africa. In Can Language Be Planned? J. Rubin and B. H. Jernudd, Eds. Hawaii: The University Press of Hawaii (East-West Center Book).

APPENDIX

SAMPLE OF 46 JOKES WITH CAPSULE TRANSLATIONS[1]

---

[1]Each joke is identified with a joke number, an author name, and an author location. Full author names are not given--only that part of the name which has been used to assign probable tribal identity. Christian names and initial are also omitted. Author locations are post office box locations, but the post office box numbers have been omitted.

Each joke is given in the same manner in which it was prepared by its author (except for being typed). There are, however, two kinds of minor alterations. Character designations for characters' speech in the exchange, and the left margins of the speech, are aligned vertically for ease of reading. In some cases, where original line lengths would have exceeded page width, lines have been shortened by moving the ends of lines back to the front of the next line. Two jokes have been extensively reorganized (15 and 21). In each case both the original and the reorganized versions are given.

Marginal clarifications (e.g. additional punctuation) are enclosed in brackets. (It should be noted that no joke author used square brackets in joke originals, although parentheses were used.) Some jokes are not direct copies of originals but are based upon typed copies made of the originals in Kenya. For these jokes only, certain probable typographical errors are pointed out by underlining the probable error and inserting the correction following it in brackets. Every fifth line number is given to the left.

Following each joke is a capsule translation. Numbers in brackets refer to line numbers. Bracketed comments are explanatory notes. A parenthesis preceded by an asterisk indicates an uncertain, but probable, translation. Double parentheses indicate an uncertain translation. Forms which are given in the translation exactly as they appeared in the joke are enclosed in quotation marks. The point of each joke is emphasized in the translation and often much subsidiary joke material is omitted. In order to maintain the flavor of the jokes (as much as is possible) colloquial English usage, and some contractions, have been used in constructing these translations.

J1 author: Abeid location: Mombasa

Siku moja Onyango alikwenda mjini kutafuta kazi, mara akaingia ndani ya duka la Patel na kuuliza kazi.
ONYANGO: Jambo mitu ya Banglades.
PATEL: Jambo bana Africa.
ONYANGO: Banakoba mimi nataka kasi.
PATEL: Ooooh! Veve kaji taka.
ONYANGO: Ndio misee.
PATEL: Veve makono ako refu fupi?
ONYANGO: Ooowi! mikono yangu mirefu Bwana.
PATEL: Oooh Bagwan! Chori kusa kuja, veve sema makon
ako refu, mimi pantaka wewe iko miji kuba!
ONYANGO: Mimi apana iko mitu ya miji mimi olitoka U.K.

[1-2] Onyango goes into town looking for work and enters Patel's shop. [8] Patel asks him if he is trustworthy [lit are his hands long or short--'long hands' meaning a thief]. [9] Onyango [not understanding and, wanting to please] responds that his hands are long. [10-11] Patel exclaims that he does not want a thief in town. [12] Onyango says he is not from town but from "U.K." [United Kisumu--a slang expression for a Luo area].

J2 author: Abulitsa location: Kisii

Mtoto mwanafunzi alienda Shuleni Siku
yake ya kwanza na Wakakutana na Mzungu, na vile
Mtoto hakuelewa Kisungu Vizuri Mambo yalikua
hivi
Mzungu: Good Morning boy!
Mtoto: Mimi si boi yako ya kukupikia
chakula jikoni!
Mzungu: How are you?
Mtoto: At ari yuu ndio Kusema nini?
Mzungu: Say fine Sir!
Mtoto: At faini ya Saa?
Basi Mtoto vile hakuelewa kizungu Kusikia
fine Sir akafikiria Mzunga amesema
atoe faini ya Saa alitimua mbio
Kama Suara mpaka nyumbani
hakurudi tena Shuleni Mpaka Sasa.

[1-3] A student starting school for the first time, who doesn't know English, meets a European teacher who [10] tells him to respond to the greeting, "How are you?", with "Fine Sir". [11-16] The child thinks he is being fined [i.e. punished] and runs home and still hasn't returned to school.

J3 author: Aluda location: Nairobi

TAJIRI ALIYE KOSA KULIPA KODI YASITIMA ALIKOSA CHAKULA CHAMUCHANA, NAALIPOFIKA KWAKE NYUMBANI MAMBO YALIKUWA HIVI BAINA YAKE NA MPISHI WAKE:

TAJIRI: Wapi chakula chamchana?
MPISHI: Nasitika leo utaonjia njia?
TAJIRI: Unasema kitugani wewe?
MPISHI: Nasema leo hutaweza kula chakula cha mchana hapa.
TAJIRI: Mbona?
MPISHI: Kwasababu hakuna stima.
TAJIRI: Kwani leo imeanda wapi.
MPISHI: Wenye stima wameikata.
TAJIRI: Mbona wakaikata?
MPISHI: Kwakuwa hukukumbuka kulipa pesa.
TAJIRI: Kwasababu gani hukunipigia simu unijulishe?
MPISHI: Kumbe umesahau yakua umefunga simu yako?
TAJIRI: Si ungepiga kutoka kwa rafiki?
MPISHI: Akili ya rafiki yako ni mbovu kama yako.
TAJIRI: Ukirudia kusema hivyo tena utawatha kazi.
MPISHI: Sasa unaweza Kukumbuka kufuta mimi kazi nasio kuli Pesa yawenyewe.
TAJIRI: Nipe maji yamachungua niende kazini.

[1-3] An employer [Tajiri] has not paid his electric bill and the electricity has been turned off so that the cook cannot prepare lunch. The cook tells him that [9] there is no electricity [stima], that [11] it was turned off because [13] he did not pay, and that [15] he could not call because the employer locks his phone. [17] The cook also says he could not use the neighbor's phone because he is as foolish [i.e. also locks his phone] as the employer. [18] The employer threatens to fire the cook and [19-20] the cook responds that you can remember to fire but not to pay your debts. [21] The employer says give me some orange drink so I can return to work.

J4 author: Ayanga location: Nairobi

Siku moja katika shule fulani mambo yalikuwa hivi waka mwalimu alipomuuliza mwanafunzi wake swali:

Mwalimu: Peter, waweza kuwaambia wenzako maana ya neno hili - 'Mla watu'

Peter: Nasikitika mwalimu hata sijawahi kulisikia ne hilo.

Mwalimu: Ebu jaribu kufikiri. Najua waweza kukisia. Kwa mfano il[k]iwa utawala wazazi wako yaani na mama yako, watu watakuitaje?

Peter: Wataniiita YATIMA!

[1-2] At school a teacher asks a question of his student, [3-4] what is the meaning of cannibal. [5-6] The student [Peter] says he does not know. [7-9] The teacher, trying t get Peter to think of the word cannibal, asks Peter what he would be called if he ate his parents. [10] Peter says he would be called an orphan.

J5 author: Barazah location: Kitale

Alfred alikuwa akimtongoza msichana Mukoya hukuakiwa na Moyo wa Kumuoa ndipo mazungumzo yao yakawa hivi:

Alfred: Habari ya Kushinda dawa yangu ya Moyo.

Mukoya: Habari njema kabisa labda yako?

Alfred: Yangu ni njema, ijapokuwa natamani kukuoa leo bali kuna kimoja kinachonishangaza na Kunipa tatizo Moyoni.

Mukoya: Ni nini hayo mpenzi.

Alfred: Sitakuficha mpenzi wangu bali hayo ni kulipa mahari. Kwani kwenu mnalipa mahari chungu nzima, Mnalipa Ng'ombe kumi na nane, blanketi, kabuti, shillingi elfu, na kadhalika hata na kofia pia?

Mukoya: Hayo yote sio juu yangu bali yalianza jadi za babu wetu.

Alfred: Ukiwa Unanipenda kweli na Unataka nikuu[o]e, nenda Kwenu kwa wazazi wako uwaulize ke[a]ma wanaweza nikakuoe bure kwani mimi ndiye nitakaekulisha na kukuweka.

Mukoya: Hujui kuwa ni lazima Ulipe kwani utakuwa Umenunua blanketi la maisha, na nitakuzalia watoto tena.

Alfred: Kumbuka mimi blanketi yako, nawe yangu, na watoto ni wetu wote, Basi iliwa ni kukununua lazima nawe uninunue.

Mukoya: Sio hivyo lakini acha niende kuuliza jambo hili.

[1-2] Alfred wants to marry [seduce] Mukoya but says [9-12] that he cannot afford the brideprice. [22-24] He tries to convince Mukoya that since they will support each other in life they should each pay something [in effect, not pay anything]. [25] Mukoya goes home to ask her parents.

J6 author: Chumba location: Lessos

Kimaru alipokwenda kwa duga bulani
Kununua shukari Ali ulisa hivi
Kwa tuga la bwana David:
Kimaru: Nataka Sugaru kilo Monja
David: Thabathali Bwana Akuna Gramu Amsini alabu
najaa Gramu Elbu Monja
Kimaru: Gramu ni nini? bwana Mimi nataka
Sugaru Abana kutaka Gramu
David: Abana kusikia ati akuna Gramu. Mimi
nakusema akuna Gramu ya kubima Sugaru.
Kimaru: Aisuru Kwaeri tutakionana Siku-
ingine!!

[1-3] Kimaru goes to David's store to buy one kilo of sugar. [5-6] David says *(he only has 50 "gramu" [grams]). [7-8] Kimaru says he doesn't know "gramu", he came to buy sugar. [In effect, Kimaru is ignorant of the metric system]. [9-10] David says there are no grams to weigh the sugar [possible that shopkeeper thinks that in order to weigh out one kilogram he needs a 1000 gram weight]. [11-12] Kimaru says he will come again.

J7 author: Frank location: Nairobi

Bwana Otugo alikwenda hospitali kutaka kutibiwa, na
Daktari alipokuwa akimhoji, Otugo alimweleza ugonjwa wak
Daktari: Jina lako nani?
Otugo: Jina lake Otugo.
Daktari: Unaumwa wapi?
Otugo: Tumbo nauma, kichwa nahara damu, muguu
natemekatemeka awesi kwenda.
Daktari: Ugonjwa huu ulikuanza lini?
Otugo: Aliwanza keso bwana.

[1-2] Onyango goes to the hospital and tells the doctor [in grammatically confused Swahili] that [6-7] his stomach is hurting, his head has diarrhoea, and [9] he got sick tomorrow.

J8 author: Githinji location: Karatina

Ilikuwa jumapili Bw. Mwangi akaenda kanisani alipofika kanisani akaingia na akaketi chini. Ndipo aliamuka na kumwendea patere nakumuliza.
Mwangi: patere unakura nini?
Patere: Haya ni mambo ya Mungu.
Mwangi: Kumbe Mungu alikwambia Uwe ukina peke yako?

[4] Mwangi asks the Catholic priest what he is eating [during communion]. [5] The priest says it is things of God. [6] Mwangi asks if God told the priest that he could eat it all by himself. [In effect, Mwangi is treating communion as a meal and chiding the priest for eating by himself which is against African hospitality.]

J9 author: Hashil location: Mombasa

Mzee alimuona mtoto wa jirani yake amechukua karatasi imefungwa vitu akamuuliza hivi:
Mzee: Kombo! Umechukua nini?
Kombo: Nimechukua maini.
Mzee: Huna hishima wewe mimi nakuuliza umechukua nini wewe wanijibu maini.
Kombo: Sasa nikudanganyie nini, na mimi ninatoka sokoni nimetumwa maini.
Mzee: Watoto wa sasa hawana heshima kweli utanitambua kwa mzee wako.
Kombo: Kwani sikujui hata nikutambue kwa baba yangu.
Mzee: Huko utanijua mimi ni nani
Kombo: Hata sasa nakujua wewe ni Mzee Hasani.

[1-3] Old man asks a neighbor child [Kombo] what he is carrying and then [5-6] rebukes the child for saying "maini" [liver]. [7-8] The child says why should I lie since I've just come from the store. [9-10] Old man says children today have no manners and that he will tell his father and then the child [13] will know who the old man is. [14] The child says I know who you are, you're Mzee Hasani.

J10 author: Bulemi location: Kakamega

Mzungu kabla ya kulala, ulimuita mpishi wake na mazungumzo yakaanza hivi:

Mzungu: Kesho amka asubuhi saana. Piga sisi kofi motomoto ya Kutosha. Piga mimi Kofi tatu, memsafu kofi mbili, na watoto Oliver na Judith kofi moja moja. Sikia wewe?

Bulemi: Lajini Pwana, Mugono wangu umejomeka na hauna nguvu ya Kumpiga wode Sawasawa. Sijabiga Msungu gwa hivyo, nitadumia rungu, na nitasikia kilio ja Kisungu.

Mzungu: You bager! Nilisema upige sisi koofi ama kaafi yaani "some coffee" kiila mtu vikombe nilivyosema. Leo nimeku - suck off!

Maelezo:

Kiswahili cha mpishi ni matamshi ya kiluhya kama

Lakini-Lajini

Umejomeka - Umechomeka

Wode - Wote

Msungu - Mzungu. na kadhalika

[3-6] European tells cook to "piga kofi" for the European and his family [European means make coffee]. Cook thinks he means beat them [Swahili for slap is "kofi"] and [7-9] tells European that he isn't too strong to beat them all unless he can go get his stick. [11-13] The European yells at Bulemi and tells him what he really wanted and [profanely?] dismisses him. [Following the joke [14-19] is the author's explanation of Bulemi's Luhya accent.]

J11 author: Kabaka location: Nairobi

Bwana Onyango Alihudhuria Misa na Masungumzo yao na Padri yakawa hivi:

Padri: Bwana Mungu anena'Nyie Mliye nashida Njooni kwangu.

Onyango: Ndiyoo Padre Mtu kama mimi iko na sida mingi.

Padri: Mungu asema wenye shida, basi ikiwa watafuta kazi, ama una magonjwa jitokeze nami nitakuombea.

Onyango: Tafadhali Padre, Mungu mnyewe Office yake iko wapi?

Padri: Office yake ni hapa.

Onyango: Na Mungu Mnyewe iko wapi?

Padri: Hatuwezi kumuona. Bali tuna mwamini.

Onyango: Wolololo! Oh! Omera Wenasema si apana weza kuona yeye, Lakini mimi alikuwa nataka kuona yeye mnyewe Pasonal,-Na koeleza ye sida yangu, akuna ata nyemba ya kolala!

In church Onyango hears Catholic priest say that [3] all who are troubled and [5-6] out of work should come to God. Onyango asks the priest [7] if the church is God's office and [9] if he can see God [about work]. When priest says [11] we can't see God but can pray to him, Onyango is [12-15] greatly disappointed since he is even without a place to sleep.

J12 author: Kassim location: Maragoli

Eliud alimtuma baba yake amununulie betri za Radio na akamwambia anunue makaa ya Radio.
Eliud- Baba ni wakati gani utaenda Madukani nikutume?
Baba- Hata sasa niko naondoka.
Eliud- Basi hizi pesa ununue makaa ya Everedy.
(Baba akafika kwa duka la Joswa.)
Baba- Nipe makaa.
Joswa- Zunguka nyuma uyachague.
Baba- Gunia ni bei gani?
Joswa- Shilingi tano. (Baba akapeleka gunia la makaa nyumbani.)
Eliud- Mbona hukuyanunua makaa yaa Radio niliyo-kutuma?
Baba- Si ulisema ninunue makaa hii.
Eliud- Hukusikia vizuri nilisema ya Radio, rudi tena umwambie mwenye duka akupe betri nyekundu za Radio.
Baba- Ooh! Ulisema ile betri nyekundu? nina-ijua mbona hukusema betri ukasema makaa. Akiba haiozi tutaota hii.

[6] Eliud sends his father to get "makaa ya Everedy" [meaning batteries] for his radio, but [7-12] the father comes back with charcoal ["makaa" means charcoal in Swahili] which he bought at Joswa's store. [13-14] When son asks why, and [16-18] tells his father he wanted "betri", the father replies that [19-21] he should have said he wanted batteries ["betri"] and anyway the charcoal will be used.

J13 author: Kattanga location: Mombasa

Baba alimuuliza mtoto wake wa miaka sita maana ya O.T.C. ambayo huonekana katika magari.
Baba- Nini maana ya O.T.C.
Mtoto- O.T.C. Maana yake ni Onyango Toka Chooni.

[1-4] A father asks his young child the meaning of "O.T.C." which is on many cars. [5-6] Child tells him "Onyango toka chooni". [Onyango come out of the bathroom.] [O.T.C. stands for "Overseas Trading Co.". The child makes up the other phrase.]

J14 author: Oduma location: Taveta

Hapa ni Shamba la Mkonge. Siku moja Mtu mmoja alikuja kutafuta Kazi ya kukata Mkonge. Na Kumbuka ya kuaamba hapa ukishandikiwa kazi ya kukata Mkonge. Unapewa kisu na ifikapo Mwisho wa mwezi. Unakatwa pesa ya Kisu kwa msahara yako. MAMBO YAKAWA HIVI:

Ongaro: Bwana mimi nataka kazi ya kukata Mkonge.
Mzungu: Unajua kazi ya kukata mkonge?
Ongaro: Ndio nimekwisha kata huko MWATATE SISAL ESTATE.
Mzungu: Haya basi hiko kazi, sasa kwenda sitoo ukate kisu huko.
Ongaro: Mimi sijui kukata kisu, najua kukata mkonge tu. Kisu naweza kukata kisu namna gani? Mimi bado kuona kazi hiyo.
Mzungu: Hapana mimi nasema kwenda kwa sitoo, huko utapata Karani atapewa wewe kisu, lakini pesa yako atakata siku ya msahara yako unasikia?
Ongaro: Hala kumbe namna hiyo, hiyo mzuri tu, H[N]asikia sasa maneno.

[6] Ongaro applies for work cutting sisal. [9] He is told by the European manager [in grammatically confused Swahili] to go to the clerk and "ukate kisu" [European means [2-4] he will get a knife [kisu] and have its cost cut from his salary]. Ongaro thinks he is supposed to cut "kisu" ["knife" in Swahili] and [11-13] tells the manager he doesn't know how to do this. [14-16] The manager explains what he meant and [17-18] Ongaro understands.

J15 author: Kazungu location: Kilifi

Bwana Mramba alikutana na
Bwana Marua asikari na mambo
yakawa hiivi: Marua ako simama:
Mramba mimi: asikari ndio wewe kwani iko
mthuingine: Mramba alisimama.
Marua alipofika unakwenda-
wapi: nakwenda nyumbani. Maana-
ikuwa saatatu usiku asikari wewe
nikuwa narara wapi Mramba nyumbaya-
ngu iko Majengo ndikonilalako
asikari thoakothi Mramba ana-
toa koti alilo vaa: asikari unatoa kothi
gani una thaka kunipika?
Mramba akalishwa kofi na kasema ki
kwao (ala! mbonawe) Marua: una thukana
mimi akamlisha lingine nakutia
mkono mfukoni ambamo alipata
chetichakodi alimrudishi naku mpa-
teke aka mwambia kwenda na ha
pana angaria nyuma.
mbonawe (vipi wewe)

J15 (reorganized version)

Bwana Mramba alikutana na Bwana Marua asikari
na mambo yakawa hiivi:
Marua ako simama:
Mramba mimi:
asikari [Marua] ndio wewe kwani iko mthuingine:
Mramba [(]alisimama[)]
Marua [(]alipofika[)] unakwenda-wapi:
[Mramba] nakwenda nyumbani.
[(]maana-ikuwa saatatu usiku[)]
asikari [Marua] wewe nikuwa narara wapi
Mramba nyumbaya-ngu iko Majengo ndikonilalako
asikari [Marua] thoakothi
Mramba [(]anatoa koti alilo vaa:[)]
asikari Marua unatoa kothi gani una thaka
kunipika?
Mramba [(]akalishwa kofi na kusema [)] ki kwao
(ala! mbonawe)
Marua: una thukana mimi [(]akamlisha lingine
nakutia mkono mfukoni ambamo alipata
chetichakodi alimrudishi naku mpa-
teke aka mwambia [)] kwenda na ha pana
angaria nyuma.
[(]mbonawe (vipi wewe)[)]

[1-3] One evening, Mr. Mramba is stopped by Policeman Marua. [12] Marua asks for Mramba's "kothi" [tax receipt--standard form is kodi], but [13] Mramba gives him his "koti" [coat]. [16-22] Marua kicks Mramba, checks his tax papers and tells him to go. [Author's handwriting is difficult to read.]

J16 author: Kibera location: Nairobi

Hivi ndivyo majadiliano yalivyok[u]wa Baina ya vijana wawili walipofungwa ukurasa wa pili wa BARAZA:

Kibira: Bosi gani huyu ambaye hakosi kuwa kwenye gazeti hili la BARAZA, ukurasa wa pili?

Abuyeka: Huyu ni Mhariri thabiti wa gazeti hili tukufu.

Kibira: Mhariri huyo kazi yake hasa nini?

Abuyeka: Kazi yake hasa ni uchunguzi wa vituko na makala mengi mengineyo. Kwa jumla yeye ni baba wa vituko, Mashairi na wandishi wengine kama wa Cheka na BARAZA.

Kibira: Basi namwembea baba huyu kila la heri katika uchungizi wake.

Kibira and Abuyeka, two teenagers, have just finished reading page 2 of Baraza [Editor's page] and tell each other that this part of Baraza is enjoyable, and that the entire paper and its editor is wonderful.

J17 author: Kimbio location: Kakamega

Mzee alijinunulia hot-pants huku kadhani nguo za wanaume. Basi kaenda kutembeya huku ameivaa. Msichana mmoja kuona vili, kaanza kucheka yule mzee. Mzee naye kajisemea huyu ni mmoja wa wale wate hucheka watu nami nita mukomesha. Mzee akaanza kucheka huku anamufwata yule msichana nyuma naye msichana kaanza kulia. Lo! watu wakafa na kicheko, huku wanamucheka yule mzee na hot-pants pia huku yule msichana akichekwa na yule mzee.

[1-4] An old man buys some "hot pants" for himself thinking they are for men. [5-6] A young woman laughs at him on the street and [7-11] he turns and starts laughing at her. [12-13] She starts crying, and [13-17] all the people turn around and laugh at both of them.

J18 author: Kimutai location: Kericho

Kiplangat ni dereva ya Baniani moja Siku moja walienda safari ya kwenda Uganda Chakula yao alikua ni ya kibaniani pamoja na Kiplangat Kufika huku mambo ikawa hivi:

Baniani: Veve Kiplangat chora majii-e, alavu dengenech kari yangu machuri-e alavu veve chukua chakul

Kiplangat: Leo nakwelesa wasi kabisa, Sikutaki chakula yenu leo kabisa!

Baniani: kwa nini veve siba iko!

Kiplangat: apana tumbo yangu na kwisha ripika, nyinyi namupo mimi pilipili pilipili kila siku na nyinyi na kula pitu musuri musuri

Baniani: Sasa veve nataka nini?

Kiplangat: Nataka shillingi tano nikulie ukali na masiwa tu! Miapana pendana na pilipili.

[1-3] A Baniani [Hindu] and his driver Kiplangat go on a trip to Uganda. When they arrive the Baniani [6-7] tells Kiplangat to prepare their [common] food but [11-13] he says he can't stand to eat peppers any more and says [15-16] he wants 5 shillings to go eat porridge and milk.

J19 author: King'asia location: Kimilili

Mzungu mmoja alikuwa akichunguza Shamba lake la nyazi ndipo akamwona Wenani akipita katika Shamba lake akifanya makanyako ndipo alimsimamisha na kuanza kumwuliza jina, Mzungu alikasirika kwa kufikiri kwamba ni mchezo, kumbe jina lake lilikuwa Wenani, baada ya kuambiwa na mfanyi kazi mmoja kwamba yeye huitwa vile ndipo mambo yakawa hivi:

Mzungu: Wewe unatoka wapi?
Wenani: Mimi anatoka kwangu.
Mzungu: Unakwenda wapi?
Wenani: Ninakwenda kwangu.
Mzungu: Kwanini unafanya makanyako katika Shamba la Bwana.
Wenani: Mimi anakanyaka kwenda kwangu apana kanyaka Bwana.
Mzungu: Jina lako nani?
Wenani: Jina langu We-nani.
Mzungu: Ninasema wewe nani?
Wenani: Mimi We-nani.
Mzungu: Kwenda zako upesi nitakushitaki.
Wenani: Afwande.

[1-3] A European farmer accosts Wenani who is on his property. [13,15] When he asks Wenani his name, "Jina lako nani", and [14,16] Wenani says I am "We-nani", the European [4-5] thinks Wenani is mocking him and gets angry, [17] ordering him off his land. [wenani is also short for wewe nani, who are you?]

J20 author: Kinuthia Mbogo location: Nairobi

Mama, mtoto wake, na mwalimu. Mtoto amdanganya mwalimu:
Mama: Mtoto wangu, leo usiende shuleni sababu nitakutuma sokoni ukaniuzie sukuma-wiki.
Mtoto: Na kwani kesho Mwalimu si atanipiga kwa kukosa kwenda skuli?
Mama: Utamdanganya ulikuwa mgonjwa.
Mwalimu: Mtoto, kuja hapa nikupige!! Ulikuwa wapi jana?
Mtoto: Nilikuwa sokoni kuuza sukuma wiki.
Mwalimu: Na kwa sababu hiyo ndiyo hu-kuja skuli?
Mtoto: Mama yangu aliniambia ati nikundanganye ati nilikuwa mgonjwa.
Mwalimu: Mama yako alikwambia unindanganye? Kwenda ambia mama yako aje hapa.
Mama: Jambo mwalimu, wani-itia nini?
Mwalimu: Kwa nini ulimwambia mtoto wako anindanganye?
Mama: Sore mwalimu nisamehe huyo mtoto wangu ni mjinga, si yeye alikundanganya.

[2-3] A mother tells her child not to go to school but to help her at the market. [4-5] Child asks how will he not be beaten, [6] and mother says tell the teacher you were sick. [10-11] The next day the child instead tells the teacher that his mother had told him to lie, [12-13] and the teacher calls in the mother [16-17] who apologizes by saying that her child is a fool and is not at fault.

J21 author: Kisu location: Mombasa

Kulikua na Mzungu na bibi wake na mfanyi kazi
siku moja bibi wa Mzungu alisafiri akabaki mfanyikazi
na Mzungu wa aiume, Mzungu akamuita mfanyikazi Jon.
(5) kuya haba. Jon: haya nimekuja bwana. Mzungu: leo utapika
nini kwamimi wee jua pikapika. Jon: nitajaribu.
(10) Mzungu: leo pika kukupaka. Jon: haya bwana.
Mzungu alikua, ana fuga paka lake kuwa kibande cha
pusi. Mzungu akaenda zake kazini. Jon akaanza kufukuza lile pande la paka maramoja akalishika akalichinja
(15) na kupika vitu vyote vikawa tayali saa 5 Mzungu
kaingia akaketi kungojea saa 6 ifike ndipo ale.
Mzungu anatupa macho huku na huku paka halioni kilasiku
akiingia hulikuta mlangoni. saa imefika akawekewa
chakula mezani kuziona akagutu lakini akasema nitauliza
(20) bada ya kushiba. Tayali ameshiba anatafuta paka wake
ampe nyama akaita Jon nam. Paka yangu yuwapi.
Jon akajibu: si hiyo unakula. Mzungu: nani na chinja.
(25) Jon: mimi. Bwana: mimi nakula paka yangu maigodi
mmmmmm majiga wewe pika paka yangu mimi kula
mamsapu kuya hapa piga gumi moja wewe ona nywele
(30) yangu naanza toka moyamoya kama majani ya miti
gozi nawekawapi mimi taka tengeneza kofia ya pusi
yangu na wewe kazi hakuna kwenda jako
kama chelewa chelewa wewe pata gumi moja
(35) ya mamsapu. Jona akatoka na kukimbia mbio.

Note: line numbers in parentheses refer to line numbers on reorganized version below.

J21 (reorganized version)

Kulikua na Mzungu na bibi wake na mfanyi kazi[.] siku moja bibi wa Mzungu alisafiri akabaki mfanyikazi na Mzungu wa kiume. Mzungu akamuita mfanyikazi Jon.

[Mzungu:] kuya haba.
Jon: haya nimekuja bwana.
Mzungu: leo utapika nini kwamimi wee jua pikapika.
Jon: nitajaribu.
Mzungu: leo pika kukupaka.
Jon: haya bwana.

[(]Mzungu alikua, ana fuga paka lake kuwa kibande cha pusi. Mzungu akaenda zake kazini, Jon akaanza kufukuza lile pande la paka maramoja akalishika akalichinja na kupika vitu vyote vikawa tayali saa 5 Mzungu kaingia akaketi kungojea saa 6 ifike ndipo ale. Mzungu anatupa macho huku na huku paka halioni kilasik akiingia hulikuta mlangoni, saa imefika akawekewa chakula mezani kuziona akagutu lakini akasema nitauliz bada ya kushiba. Tayali ameshiba anatafuta paka wake ampe nyama akaita Jon nam.[)]

Mzungu: Paka yangu yuwapi.
Jon: [(]akajibu[)] si hiyo unakula.
Mzungu: nani na chinja.
Jon: mimi.
Bwana[Mzungu]: mimi nakula paka yangu maigodi mmmmmm majiga wewe pika paka yangu mimi kula mamsapu kuya hapa piga gumi moja wewe ona nywele yangu naanza toka moyamoya kama majani ya miti gozi nawekawapi mimi taka tengeneza kofia ya pusi yangu na wewe kazi hakuna kwenda jako kama chelewa chelewa wewe pata gumi moja ya mamsapu.

[(]Jona akatoka na kukimbia mbio.[)]

[1-3] European's wife leaves on a trip leaving him and their cook, Jon. [7-8] European tells Jon [in grammaticall confusing Swahili] to cook something for him and [10] to cook chicken for his cat [European says "pika kukupaka"-- lit. cook chicken cat]. [12-20] Jon cooks the cat for supper and the European eats it and [26-34] becomes enraged when he asks where the cat is and learns he has eaten it. [35] Jon runs away.

J22 author: MacMajale location: Kerugoya

Katika skuli moja mwalimu mkuu wa skuli hiyo alikua akishi na mwanafunzi moja aitwaye Nang'ayo. Kila siku Nang'ayo ndiye alikua anafanyia Mwalimu kazi ya aina yote ya nyumbana pamoja na kutumwatumwa kila saa. Basi siku moja mambo yakawa hivi.

Mwalimu- Hebu nang'ayo kimbia sokoni ununue mboga kilo moja haraka. (akiwa na nia ya nyama.)

Nang'ayo- Ndio Mwalimu. (Nang'ayo aliendа haraka na badala ya kununua nyama alinunua kunde alafu akarudi haraka kwa Mwalimu.)

Nang'ayo- Nimerudi Mwalimu. nimepata mboga safi sana.

Mwalimu- Asante sana basi saa ya chakula cha mchana iko karibu kwa hivyo enda ukate ya kutosha alafu uweke kwa seng'enge uchome na upikie ugali ya kutosha Nitakuja na walimu wenzangu kwa chakula.

Nang'ayo- Ndio Mwalimu. (Nang'ayo alienda alafu akachukuwa kunde aka-weka kwenye sang'enge na kuchoma alafu akaweka maji ya ugali. Bada ya kupika ugali ali rogota jifu ya kunde hiyo na ku-weka kwenye sahani. Saahiyo hiyo Mwalimu mkuu huyo akaingia na walimu wenzake. Walikaa alafu Nang'ayo akaleta ugali alafu akafwatisa sani ya jifu ya kunde ikiwa imefunikwa vizuri na sani yingine. Wote walisafisha makono na kufunua sani iliyekua imefunika jifu la kunde.)

Walimu Wote: Loo hi ni nini tumewekewa kwenye sani ni uchawi ni nini?

Mwalimu Mku: Hebu nang'ayo hi ni nini umetuletea? Sema haraka au nikuchape saa hii.

Nang'ayo: Hiyo si makosa yangu. Wewe uliniambia ninunue mboga si nyama. Tena ukasema badala ya kupika nichome. Sasa ningefanya nini.

Mwalimu: Hata ugeuze kiswahili yake hiyo, Funganisha vitu viako viyote na uwende ukae kwenu.

A headmaster tells Nang'ayo, [1-6] a student who also works for the headmaster, [8-10] to get and prepare "mboga" [one meaning is a meat to accompany rice]. [11-14] Nang'ayo buys beans [other meaning is vegetable] and [23-36] broils them like meat. [46-48] The headmaster dismisses him, although [42-45] Nang'ayo claims it wasn't his fault.

J23 author: Moses location: Mombasa

Baba alimpeleka Lume hospitali daktari mpe dawa hii ma
tatu kwa siku:
Baba: Ndiyo, saa ya kula kumaliza.
Baba: (Amwita) Lume!! Lume!! Lume!!
Lume: Haya baba.
Baba: (Akampa dawa.)
Mama: Hebe nione dawa gani? Aaaa!! Shake the bottle
before use.
Mama: Hebui! mshike miguu na mimi ntamshi
mikoko wakamtikisa.
Lume: Ha!! Ha!! Ha!!, mama baba nafa.

[1-6] A father gets medicine for his child Lume and at the proper time gives Lume a portion. [7-10] Mother then reads the label "shake before using" and so she and the father grab Lume and begin shaking him.

J24 author: Mugofu location: Nairobi

Rafiki: Umenunua gari gani?
Mkulima: Wustini Morrisi!
Rafiki: Ulinunu kutoka mzungu?
Mkulima: Ndio!
Rafiki: Alikuwa mwanamke?
Mkulima: Ndio!
Rafiki: Alikuwa ameolewa au memusafu tu!
Mkulima: Gari kike au kuime mimi sijui!

[1] A friend asks Mkulima what kind of car he bought. [2] He tells him an Austin Morris. [3] The friend asks if he bought it from a European, and [5] a woman. [4] Mkulima says yes. [7] The friend asks him if she/it was married or not. [8] Mkulima says he doesn't know [care] if the car is male or female.

J25 author: Mukoya location: Kisumu

Mama alipokwenda Hosipitalini kwa kujikungwa aliwacha mtoto mdogo na Yaya wake nye[u]mbani. Mama alipotoka Hosipitali maneno yakaiv[w]a Hivi:

Mtoto: Yaya! Mama amerudi kutoka Hosipitali na ametolewa mtoto kwa tumbo yake!

Yaya: Ndiyo mama amelete mtoto mzungu kutoka Hosipitali Unaweze beba huyo mtoto?

Mtoto: Hapana mimi niko mdogo. Lakini kesho mimi nitakwenda Hosipitali niwaan[m]biye watu wa Hospitali wanitohe mtoto wakunitosha mimi. Halafu mama atampa maziwa.

[4-5] A child tells Yaya, her 'nanny', that her mother is home from the hospital with a baby from her stomach. [8-11] The child says I haven't held the baby because I am small but tomorrow I will go to hospital and tell them to take from me a baby my size and then mother can give it milk.

J26 author: Wanyama location: Webuye Falls

Mama mmoja aliingia afisini mwa(Advocate) na akamukute karani Matingi, mambo yakawa hivi:

Matingi: Jambo Mama.

Mama: ee Jambo mayi.

Matingi: Nikusaidie nini Mama?

Mama: Nisaidie mameno yefwe ya ngolobe, mala yule musakhulu amekataa.

Matingi: Sema Kiswahili vizuri mama kwani mimi sisikii lugha yako vizuri, ati amekataa nini?

Mama: Ati kwa sababu paka na panya waliki mbisana wakamukata matere.

[1-2] A woman enters a law office and [6-7] tells the clerk Matingi [in Swahili mixed with Luhya] that she needs assistance because her husband has kicked her out of the house. [8-9] Matingi asks her to speak in Swahili. [10-11] She repeats by saying in Swahili literally *(the cat chased a rat) [the cat being her husband and the rat her lover].

J27 author: Mussima location: Bungoma

Baba mmoja baada ya kushoshwa na tabia mbaya za mwanawe alianza kumshauri ili aache kutenda maovu lakini palitokea zogo kali baina yao hata mtoto akazidi kumkasirisha sana babake wakati alipojaribu kumwambia hivi:

BABA: Usipoyashika haya yangu na kuacha kujichukulia sheria mikononi siku moja utakiona kilichomnyoa kanga manyoya.

MTOTO: Mimi sijachukua sheria yeyote mikononi wala sinayo kabisa mifukoni!!!

[1-2] Father is lecturing child on bad behavior. [2-4] Child becomes angry when father says [6-8] you shouldn't take the "sheria" [law] into your own hands. [9-10] Child replies that he hasn't taken any "sheria" in his hands nor in his pocket.

J28 author: Mwaiwo location: Wundanyi

Jifuze uraiya nauye ndele shida namasha ka ni kwako wewe mwenye kukosa kuji-fuzau raiya Je? ukikosa kujifuzauraiya utakuwa na maisha bora ndio urongo yako hutakuwa na maisha bora hata kidongo. jifuzeuraiya kwa mamboyote yazani nayaki-sasa. utakuwa mwana ichi mwema na raiya mwe ma. Na uta che ha ha ha hi hi hi na si si si sina shida. Shida na mashaka nikwako wewe usio juwauraiya he he he he heye twamuche-asiye jiwa uraiya furaha hata ki ndongo ni shidatu kwake. Soma baraza nauendele na uwe raiya mwena sana sana wa nchi yaa africa mashariki muchafu ni tajiri na musafi ni tajiri shida na mashaka ni kwanani shida na mashaka ni kwa mutu binafusi. Tongoza mwezio naye-akutongoze usitongozwo nausio tongoza-mapezi yote ni huku na huko. Mapezi ifwanya maisha yako iwe bora sana wa wako mzuri na ma-ridadi wamsemowako fahamu haba na haba hujaza kibaba fwa fwanga fwanga huku na huko. Bibi ni huku bwana huko. Mutoto waki ume na baba yake na mtoto kike na mama yake. Kazini pamoja.

[Seems to be a rambling statement on being a good citizen, etc. and not a 'joke'. The script, author's handwriting and punctuation is very difficult to read and the organization of the sentences is not clear.]

J29 author: Kamau Mwangi location: Nakuru

Kamau kakutana na Onyango ambaye afanya kazi Marshal
Ltd. ikawa hivi:
Kamau: Rafiki yagu wewe unafanya Kathi wafi thiku hithi?
Onyango: Mimi onfanya kabi kwa machoo.
Kamau: Ndifo nini kuona unafaa nguo shafu hivi.
Onyango: Ndio rafiki yangu. lakini chuga sana apana
ulisa mimi maswali mingi. Mimi bado pata kasi.
Mimi nakula lami na meno hata miguu.

[1-2] Kamau meets Onyango who is working at Marshall's Ltd. [4] Onyango tells him he is working with "machoo" [Marshall's, "machoo" would also refer to toilets]. [5] Kamau says I can see your dirty clothes. [6-8] Onyango says don't ask me any more questions as I have work to do. ((I am eating "lami" [?] and teeth do not have arms)).

J30 author: Mwanyika location: Taveta

Mwalimu aliwaandikia wanafunzi maneno
haya kwa ubao ili wayatafsiri katika
lugha ya Kiingereza:
"Wewe Juma kila siku unanipiga, kiila
siku unanipiga kwaniini? Toka nje leo
tupigane, na utajua mimi mwanamume
kwelikweli."
Mmoja wa wanafunzi alitafsiri hivi:
"You Juma everyday you beat me, every
day you beat me because? From out
to fight today and you will know I am
a childhusband truetrue."

Student is asked by teacher to translate a Swahili sentence into English on the blackboard. The student does a very literal, and very awkward, translation. [e.g. in line 6, "mwanamume", instead of using 'man', Juma writes it as a combination child-husband].

J31 author: Mwera location: Nairobi

Kichekesho kikubwa kilitokea majuzi wakati Songoro alipokuwa katika nyendo zake mitaani na kwa ghafla akakutana na Kisura mmoja alie kuwa nadhifu mwenye Pochi kubwa, wigi, na stoking. Baadae walielewana lugha hivyo Songoro akampeleka Hoteli ili wapate Chakula.

Songoro- Waonaje bibie?
Kipusa- Sijambo bwana.
Songoro- Naona kama nakuelewa, nadhani tulikutana zamani.
Kipusa- Pengine labda, wajua mambo ni ......
Songoro- Haidhuru utamalizia Hoteli, hebu twende tukapate mlo.

Songoro- Weita? hebu tafdhali niletee Menu. Je bibi utakula nini?
Kipusa- Hata mimi nitakula hio hio menu.
Songoro- Samahani bibi, menu sio chakula bali ni orodha ya vyakula.

[1-4] Songoro meets a [modern-looking] girl on the street. [4-10] They talk and then they go to a restaurant. [12] Songoro asks for a "menu" and then [13] asks the girl what she would like to eat. [14] She says she'll eat a "menu" too. [15-16] Songoro tells her that a "menu" is a list of foods.

J32 author: Mwivanda location: Webuye Falls

Oiro alinunua mewani ya chua, Fred alipo-
muona amevaa mazunguzo yao yakawa hivi
Oiro- Jana nilienda kwa duka fulani
nikanunua mewani hii ya chua.
Fred- Ulinunua ya chua namna gani?
Oiro- Nilinua ya chua kwa sababu macho
yangu hasioni vizuri wakati wa chua.
Fred- Yaani hufahamu neno chua, chua
ni mtu mpumbavu, ama ulinunua
kutoka kwa mtu mpumbavu?
Oiro- La, nilinua kutoka kwa duka fulani,
ukinunua mewani ya chua utakuwaje
mpumbavu.

[3-4] Oiro tells Fred he has bought sunglasses "mewani hii ya chua" [standard form for 'sun' is jua but Oiro uses "chua"]. [8-10] Fred says that Oiro does not understand "chua" which means a fool [Fred is using "chua" for the standard form juha which means 'fool']. [11-13] Oiro [not understanding] says how can you be a fool if you buy sunglasses.

J33 author: Nashon location: Nairobi

Askari polisi alimshika Sudi akiendesha baiskeli bila t

Askari: Ewe kijana, we napanda taa hakuna baskili.

Sudi: Mzee, nitapandaje taa bila baiskeli.

Askari: Sikia mitoto, wewe osiletc miswahili yako.

Sudi: Hewallah afande, sasa hebu nijaribu kuipanda ta ya chemni niliyotoka kuinunua nawe nikuachie ba

Askari: Wewe ndiye mwenye makosa. Sisi takamata wewe.

Sudi: Vipi bwana askari, mimi ninayo taa, baiskeli nd haina.

Askari: Wewe ndiyo naendesa baskili.

Sudi: Mimi sikuilazimisha ila yenyewe ndiyo iliyokuba kunibeba.

Askari: Wewe mitoto ilo sida kubwa haya kwenda.

[1] Sudi is stopped for riding a bicycle without a light. [2] The policeman mixes up his words and says you are riding a light without a bicycle ["taa bila baskili"]. [3] Sudi says that this isn't possible. [4] The policeman replies don't *(confuse matters with your Swahili). [5-6] Sudi then tries to talk his way out by saying that he will ride the chimney lantern he has just bought and the policeman can take the bicycle. [7] The policeman says I'll arrest you. [8] Sudi then says that he has a lantern but it is the bicycle which doesn't. [10] The policeman says but you were riding it. [11] Sudi says he only hitched a ride. [13] The policeman says you are too much trouble, go away.

J34 author: Kasau location: Sagana

Kiraiko alikuwa anataka kuwa tajiri, tena na mwenye akili sana. Asijue la kufanya, basi ndipo aliamua kumtafuta mganga wa kumweleza vile atafanya ndivyo afani kiwe, ni utajiri, na akili nyingi sana. Basi bila taabu yoyote, akapita kinjia hiki, na kinjia kile, mara akaona kibao kilichoandikwa "Mganga" basi akaenda kinjia kile alokoekekezwa hadi kwa mganga. Akafika, akapiga hodi, akafunguliwa, wakanza kusalimiana, mambo yakawa hivi:

[Kiraiko:] Wewe ndiye mganga?
[Mganga:] Ndiyo mimi ndiyo[e] mganga.
[Kiraiko:] Hujambo mganga?
[Mganga:] Sijambo sana, sana, uuuuh. Hebu nieleze jina l: Jina langu aaah naitwa mganga Kasumba!! na wewe:
[Kiraiko:] Aah, na mimi naitwa Kiraiko, na shida yangu nataka kuwa tajiri, na akili nyingi sana.

Basi mganga akamwambia: Sikiliza nenda mpaka nyumbani kwak(alafu chukua mbuzi yule anatwa ng'ondu, halafu panda naye juu ya paa ya choo, na uanze kumpiga na rungu mara safari nne, na ililia lia sema hivi utajiri na akili ne[a] vije.

Kiraiko akaenda mpaka nyumbani kwake. Kwa vile hakulipishw kitu, akaenda akamfungua mbuzi yule wake anayeitwa ng'ondu kuanza kupanda naye hadi juu ya paa la choo, na kuanza kaz: ya kufanya kama alivyoagiziwa na mganga. Kiraiko akanza kumpiga yule mbuzi aitwaye ng'ondu safari zile zile nne alizoagizwa na mganga, na kusema vile vile. Safari ya kwanza: Puuuh! Safari ya pili: Puuuh!! Akisema sema utajiri na akili na vije safari ya tatu Puuuuh na huku mbuzi analia na yeye anasema: Utajiri na akili na vij Safari ya nne Puuuh, muuuh, momomooh, kekekeeh pururuused muukhu mara hawo, chini, tena hawooooo ndani ya shimo la m yeye pamoja na mbuzi, pamoja, nyasi, miti, ndani woote na vyoote na huku yeye Kiraiko yungali anasema utaajiri, naa aaakili na vijeeh!

[1-4, 14-15] Kiraiko wants to be rich and smart so he goes to a "mganga" ['medicine man'], [16-19] who tells him to take his goat and climb on top of his latrine and beat the goat and yell for wealth and wisdom to come. [20-33] Kiraiko does this but the roof caves in and he falls into the latrine's pit still yelling for wealth and wisdom.

J35 author: Chege location: Gilgil

Mtu mwenye kuendesha gari la Punda Katika soko moja upa wa Limuru alifanya hivi aliendewa na rafiki wake na kumuuliza hivi:

Mtu: hei Mzee huwezi kumuogopa punda azikupige teke?
Mzee: hawezi kunipiga teke ananinjua sana.
Mtu: Panga hainjui mwenywe.
Mzee: loo loolo.
Mtu: Kitu gani?
Mzee: Punda amenipiga tekemuguu umevunjika
Mtu: umeniambia anakujua
Mzee: Sijui amefanya nini SaSa, Ni zaindie niende hospi
Mtu: Sharori yako na punda wako.

[1-2] Two men [a man and an old man] with a donkey cart on the way to the market. [4] The man says to the old man aren't you afraid the donkey will kick you. [5] He says no, it knows me. [7,9] The old man yells that the donkey has kicked him. [10] The other man says I thought the donkey knew you. [11] The old man says, never mind, take me to the hospital. [12] The man says *(that is your business with your donkey.)

J36 author: Nicholas location: Nanyuki

James alikuwa anaenda shuleni aka
pata Mzee shem anangoja basi
lakumtuba taoni Basi mambo yakawa hivi:
James- Jambo Mzee
Mzee shem- Jambo Kijana.
James- Unatabu gani Mzee
Shem- Mimi naongoja basi niende
taoni. Kwa vile mimi naona
nimbali sana siwezi fika hu
ko namiku.
Jamesi- Tuseme Ukipata Basi Utawa
ja miku hapa Mzee.
Shem- wewe ahuna adabu una
soma wapi wewe mtoto bumb
afu namna hii
James- Mimi nasoma kwa kitabu.

[1] James, on his way to school, comes upon old man Shem waiting for a bus. [8-11] Shem says he is waiting for a bus to town since it is too far by foot ["namiku"--standard is <u>na</u> <u>miguu</u>--literally, 'by/with legs']. [12-13] James asks *(suppose you get a bus will you leave your legs here) [possible that James takes 'with legs' literally]. [14-16] Shem tells James he has no manners and asks him where he learns this. [17] James says he studies books.

J37 author: Njuguna location: Ruiru

Wamangu alipoingia katika hoteli
mazungumzo yalikuwa hivi kati yake na weita:
Wamangu: Nipe, tafadhal, chai ya kijinga.
Weita: Hatuuzi hiyo, tafadhali.
Wamangu: Je! Una hakika hamuzi chai ya "cream"?
Weita: Pole sana kwa lugha. Tunauza kwa wingi.
Wamangu: Pole pia kwa ufasaha wangu wa lugha.
Hatoka pwani mie.

[1-3] Wamangu enters a restaurant and asks the waiter for "chai ya kijinga" [lit. stupid tea]. [4] The waiter says we don't sell this. [5] Wamangu exclaims What! You don't sell tea with cream? ["chai ya kijinga" also means this]. [6] The waiter says sorry for my language, we sell it. [7-8] Wamangu says excuse my purity of language, *(I come from the coast.)

J38 author: Njuguna location: Turbo

Ofisa wa elimu, akiandamana na mkaguzi wa shule (Supervisor) walizuru, na kutembelea shule moja ya msingi mnamo saa tatu za asubuhi. Alipoingia darasa la saba. alimkuta mwalimu mkuu akiwapa wana funzi hesabu za kichwa na maswali yali kuwa yanaulizwa hivi:

Mwalimu: Kila mwanafunzi lazima ajibu kwa haraka kama umeme kwa muda usio zidi nukta moja, la sivyo, ni sharti atoke nje kwa kuwa ni mjinga wa mwisho.

Rashid: Mimi niko tayari mwalimu niulize

Mwalimu: ekari moja ina square yards-ngapi Rashid?

Rashid: Ekari moja ina square yards 4840

Mwalimu: Ahasante Rashid kwa jibu lako.

Rashid: Tafadhali ewe mwalimu, Ngombe mwenye uzani wa ratili mia sita, huwa ana uzito wa "oz" ngapi, baada ya kumkata kichwa chake chenye uzani wa ratili Arobaini?

Mwalimu: [(] Alikaa kimya kwa zaidi ya dakika moja bila kutoa jibu lolote.[)]

Rashid: Nenda nje mwalimu bila kupoteza wakati wewe ni mjinga wa mwisho.

"Wanafunzi- ofisa, na supervisor- Wote wakaangua Kicheko cha ajabu"

[1-7] The Education Officer and school Supervisor are observing a Standard seven class in arithmetic being taught by the headmaster. [8-11] The teacher tells the students they must answer very quickly and if they cannot they will go outside. [12-16] Rashid answers one question correctly. [17-23] Rashid then asks the teacher a question which he cannot figure out. [24-25] Rashid then tells the teacher that he is a dunce and must go outside. [26-27] All the students and the officials laugh.

J39 author: Okindo location: Nairobi

Abdala na rafiki yake Omari walilewa sana baada ya kunywa pombe nyingi hata wakaz[s]hindwa kutembea vyema Na mambo yakawa hivi:

Abdala: Rafiki yangu Omari mbona leo tumelewa hivi.

Omari: Wewe ukinywa pombe usinywe tu hadi kooni. Tena nakuonya uache hii tak[b]ia yako ya kuuliza maswali ya Kilevi.

[1-2] Abdala and Omari are so drunk they have trouble walking. [4] Abdala asks Omari why are we so drunk. [5-6] Omari says do you think *(you only drink with your throat), and adds stop asking questions about drunkenness.

J40 author: Okutoyi location: Kwisero [Yala]

Baada ya Joyce mkewe Simon Kumaliza miaka nne bila kupata hata mtoto mmoja ilitokea siku moja alijaribu kumtanga bwana wake ya kuwa amepata mtoto kuz[s]udi asifukuzwe:

Joyce: Baada ya miaka hii yote bila Mungu kunipatia mtoto j[z]amani....... Shetani tu.

Simon: Taabu gani nawe?

Joyce: Wacha kuniuliza mume wangu yaliyonipata yamenitosha.

Simon: Umekumbukwa na Mungu au umeokota Shetanitu?

Joyce: Saa ya huzini ni huzuni si vichekesho.

Simon: Basi sema wasi yaliyokukuta.

Joyce: Nimekwenda ndani yo Choo na nilipokuwa nikitaka kukamiliza haja Kubwa mtoto ndiye aliyetoka tumboni badala yake.

Simon: Tumbo Siku hizi ni kama Mtungi ambapo mtoto kutoka ni rahisi.

Joyce: Mimi nikikumbuka mtoto wangu ninaweza. Kujinyonga.

Simon: Ha-we-ha-wa hiyo ni uongo wewe umekwenda haja Kubwa na ukadhani ati ni mtoto la sivyo unajitetea.

[1-3] Joyce has been married 4 years to Simon but hasn't given him a child. [11-13] Joyce attempts to tell Simon that she had a child so she won't be thrown out. She mourns that she thought she was having a bowel movement but instead a baby came out [and was lost]. [17-18]Simon ridicules her and doesn't believe her story.

J41 author: Ombongi location: Kisii

Nahashoni aliporudi Shuleni temu ya
pili, Kila mwanafunzi alitaka Kujua ugonjwa
uliomsumbua Kwa nyakati hizi zote zilizopita.
Wanafunzi(kwa umoja): Nini kilikusumbua namna hii?
Nahashoni (kwa huzuni): Ugonjwa wa "peritonites".
Wana[funzi]: Ugonjwa gani huu? Hatujawahi Kuusikia.
Nah[ashoni]: Wa tumbo.
Wana: Uliuponaje, kwani tulisikia pilkapilka
eti utapiga kikabu teke?
Naha: Nilipasuliwa.
Wana: Kama mbao?
Naha: Hapana, nilifanyiwa oparehe shooni.
(mmoja wa wanafunzi) Daudi: Eti Matumbo yote
yamo nje hata sasa! 'Hebu nitazame'.
toeni shati ili nami nitambue nilivyo.
Naha: (akirukwa na hasira): Una
walakin wewe? Nitakufunza
kutochecheri na watu.
(Hapo ukaanza mchavuano baina ya
Nahashoni na Daudi hapo wanafunzi
wakipiga makelele badala ya
kuhusunika na Nahashoni).

[1-2] Nahashoni returns to school [after an illness]. [2-4] The students crowd around him and ask him what he had. [5] He says he had "peritonites", and [10,12] he had an operation to be cured. [13-15] One student, Daudi, wants to see Nahashoni's stomach. [16-18] Nahashoni becomes angry, and [19-20] he and Daudi begin fighting. [20-22] The students are delighted instead of being sorry for Nahashoni.

J42 author: Omolo location: Nakuru

Siku moja bibi na bwanawe walikwa Safarini na bibi huyu alikwa amebeba mtoto na mizingo. Aliona amechoka sana, alianza Ungomvi na bwanawe kwani kazi yake ni a[n]zito kuliko za bwanae. Na mambo yakawa hivi:

Bibi: Mimi kazi yangu ni nzito kuliko yako na sasa mimi aiye nitakwa bwana na wewe uwe bibi(Na hapo akitia mtoto na mizingo chini.)

Bwana: Haya hata mimi nakubali niwe bibi yako, Na Kazi zangu yote wewe diye utakuwa ukifanya.

Bibi: Basi Chukwa huyu mtoto na mizingo hizi Ubebe na wewe ulete panga hiyo nibebe.

Bwana: Haya Chukwa panga. (Na hapo akachukwa mtoto na akamweka kwa mngongo na kumfunga kwa suka na mizingo akaweka kwa kichwa).

Bibi: Sasa tuanze Safari na utembee haraka kwani tunataka tufike nyumbani haraka. (Na wakati bibi alipokwa mbele alikutana na nyoka kubwa sana na yeye badala ya kumuua nyoka huyo alipiga nayowe na Kurundi nyuma kwa bwana yake.

Bwana: Si wewe diye ulisema kwamba kazi yangu ni rahisi basi muue huyo nyoka.

Bibi: (akitetemeka) lete mtoto na mizingo na wewe uchukwe panga yako, ufanye kazi hiyo.

Bwana: Sasa unaona kazi ya wanaume si rahisi, kwa sababu nyoka huyu pengine inaweza kuniua. (na akaenda akamuua nyoka huyo.)

[1-3] During a trip, the wife thinks her husband's work is easy. [5-7] She sets down her load and child and demands that he should do her work and she his. [8-9] The husband agrees. [16-19] The wife goes ahead with the husband's machete until she sees a big snake, then she runs and [22-23] wants to change back. [24-25] The husband says now you know that men's work is not easy.

J43 author: Mohamed location: Mombasa

Kijana mumo akikuwa akichapwa na mama yake, kila akojowapo kitandani mpaka akawacha. Siku moja kwa bahati mbaya alikojowa kitandani na mambo yakawa hivi:

Mama: Leo umekojowa tena basi utakiona cha mtema kuni.
Mumo: (akijitetea)"Tafadhali mama mimi sikukojowa bali ni kitanda ndicho kilicho kojowa."
Mama: (akishangaa) kitanda hukojowa?
Mumo: Ndiyo, kwa sababu mimi nikienda kukojowa mchana huwa hakitaki kunifuata tukojowe sote, bali hungoja usiku tu ndiyo kikojowe, nami nataka ukichape kama unavyo nichapa mimi ili kisikojowe tena....

[1-2] Mumo is beaten when he wets his bed. [3-4] He does it again and [6-7,9-12] tries to plead with his mother that the bed itself had urinated not him and that mother should beat the bed.

J44 author: Tsumah location: Mombasa

Mamaake Ali alikuwa mgonjwa sana wa T.B. siku nyingi na bila kupona. Sasa babaake Ali, akamtuma Ali kupige Bao kwa mganga ili ajue kiini cha ugonjwa huo.

Baba: Nenda kule ng'ambo ya ule mto ukapige bao kwa mganga.

Ali: [(]Alikwenda mpaka kwenye Nyumba ya mganga huku akishikilia gongo mkononi. Akaliona Bao moja ambalo liko karibu na nyumba ya mganga na kuanza kulipiga.[)] (mganga mwenyewe alikuwa ndani ya nyumba. Akasikia bao lake la kakalia huko nje lapigwa kwa gongo, akatoka nje na kumrukia Ali).

Mganga: Mbona wapiga bao langu hapa nje? Hujui kwamba utalivunja?

Ali: Baba yangu ameniambia niende kupiga bao kwa mganga. Na sasa mganga ndio wewe, ndio maana napiga hili Bao lako.

Mganga: Hapana, yeye hakukwambia uje upige bao la mti lililo karibu na nyumba yangu. Mimi najua yeye anataka bao la uganga.

Ali: Basi nifanyie bao la uganga.

Mganga: (Akapiga bao lake kwa kutumia vyombo vya kiganga na kumwambia Ali) 'Kweli ile ni T.B. lakini hapa kwetu hakuna mganga wake. Kwa hivyo yataka uende Ng'ambo kwenye waganga wenye ujuzi.

Ali: [(]Aliporudi Nyumbani akamweleza yale ya mganga.[)]

Baba: Basi nenda mpaka ofisi ya Forodhani akachukue Pasi ya mamaako aende Ng'ambo

Ali: [(]akaenda mpaka Ofisi ya Forodhani. Akaangalia akoano duka upande wa pili wa ile ofisi. Akanunua Pasi la kupigia nguo na kumpelekea Babaake.[)]

Baba: Silo pasi hili. Nataka kile kitambulisho cha kuonyesha mtu aende ng'ambo, ambacho hupatikana kwenye Ofisi za Forodha. Kitambulisho hiki huitwa Pasi au Pasipoti.

[1-2] Ali's mother is very sick with "T.B.". [2-3,4-5] Ali's father sends him to a mganga ('medicine man') to "piga bao" [idiom for divining, Ali thinks it is literally: beat a tree]. [6-8] Ali goes and beats on a tree next to the mganga's house. [9-11,17-19] The mganga comes out and explains to Ali what "piga bao" means. [21-25] He also tells Ali that they must send his mother overseas. [28-29] Ali is then sent to the immigration office by his father to get a "pasi" [meaning passport] for his mother. [30-32] Instead he comes back with a clothes iron [other meaning of pasi].

J45 author: Waiganjo location: Nairobi

Bi Agnes alikuwa akitafuta mahali pa kukaa ndani ya basi yenye orofa iliyokuwa imejaa. Kwa bahati akamwo rafiki yake Wamboi na wakaanza kuongea.

Agnes: Waenda wapi dada.
Wamboi: Naenda town kununua nguo
Agnes: (Kwa mshangao) Ah! umekosea dada. teremka kwenye basi la chini. Hili la juu linakwenda industial area (Kwa furaha, bi Agnes akakaa)

[1-5] Agnes is looking for a place to sit on a crowded bus going to town when she sees Wamboi. [6] She asks her where she is going. [7] Wamboi says to town. [8-11] Agnes says get off, this bus is going to the industrial area. [11-12] (Agnes then sits down [in Wamboi's seat]).

J46 author: Wanyuttu location: Ruiru

Mama mmoja alimtuma mwanawe Ali kwenye duka la viatu vya bata akanunue viatu, Nyumbani mlikuwa na bata mzinga. Mambo yakawa hivi:

Mama: Ali.

Ali: Ee mama.

Mama: Shika hizi shilingi hamsa ishirini ukanunue viatu vya bata.

Ali: Ati umesema ni hamsa ishirini mama?

Mama: Ndio.

Ali: Hizo zote, shilingi sabini ni za viatu vya bata?

Mama: Shika nenda haraka sana.

Ali: Ah! mama hizi ni ishirini na tano tu, si sabini.

Mama: Shukua hizo ukimbie haraka.

Ali: Habari mwenye duka.

Mwenye duka: Nzuri.

Ali: Mimi nataka viatu vya bata, unazo?

Mwenye duka: Ndio wataka namba ngapi na rangi gani?

Ali: Sikumwuliza mama bata wetu huvaa namba ngapi wala rangi?

Mwenye duka: Ni vyako au ni yva bata?

Ali: Hebu niende kumpima bata wetu nione ni namba ngapi atavaa na rangi gani.

Mwenye duka: Subiri kidogo, mimi huuza viatu vinavyo tengenezwa na kampuni ya bata wala si viatu vya bata.

[1-2,6-7] Ali is sent by his mother to buy some "Bata" [a brand of shoe; also means duck] shoes. [19] The shoe salesman asks for size and color. [20-21] Ali says he doesn't know what size the ducks need nor what color they would like. [23-24] He says he will go find out what the ducks need. [25-27] The salesman says we sell Bata shoes not shoes for ducks.

FOREIGN AND COMPARATIVE STUDIES PROGRAM
Maxwell School of Citizenship and Public Affairs
Syracuse University
119 College Place
Syracuse, N.Y. 13210

PUBLICATIONS

AFRICAN STUDIES

II.	The Conflict Over What Is To Be Learned in Schools: A History of Curriculum Politics in Africa. 1971. 113 pp. $4.50	Stephen P. Heyneman
IV.	Foreign Conflict Behavior and Domestic Disorder in Africa. 1971. 128 pp. $4.50	John N. Collins
V.	The Politics of Indifference: Portugal and Africa, A Case Study in American Foreign Policy. 1972. 41 pp. $2.50	John A. Marcum
VIII.	The Zimbabwe Controversy: A Case of Colonial Historiography. 1973. 142 pp. $4.50	David Chanaiwa
IX.	The Union of Tanganyika and Zanzibar: A Study in Political Integration. 1973. 114 pp. $4.50	Martin Bailey
X.	The Pattern of African Decolonization: A New Interpretation. 1973. 123 pp. $4.50	Warren Weinstein John J. Grotpeter
XI.	Islamization Among the Upper Pokomo. 1973. 166 pp. $5.50.	Robert L. Bunger, Jr.
XII.	Protest Movements in Colonial East Africa: Aspects of Early African Response to European Rules.	Robert Strayer Edward I. Steinhart Robert Maxon
XIII.	Education for What? British Policy Versus Local Initiative. 1973. 100 pp. & viii. $4.50	Charles H. Lyons Kenneth J. King Richard D. Heyman John M. Trainor
XIV.	Ethnicity in Contemporary Africa. 1973. 59 pp. & vi. $3.50.	Robert H. Bates
XV.	Class and Nationalism in South African Protest: The South African Communist Party and the "Native Republic," 1928-34. 1973. 67 pp. $3.50.	Martin Legassick
XVI.	Africans in European Eyes: The Portrayal of Black Africans in 14th and 15th Century Europe. 1975. 98 pp. $4.50	Peter A. Mark

African Studies (continued)

XVII.	Drought, Famine and Population Movements in Africa. 1975. 144 pp. & vi. $4.50.	James L. Newman, Editor
XVIII.	Technology for Ujamaa Village Development in Tanzania. 1975. 64 pp. $3.50.	David J. Vail
XIX.	Citizenship in Africa: The Role of Adult Education in the Political Socialization of Tanganyikans, 1891-1961. 1975. 119 pp. $4.50.	Joel C. Millonzi
XX.	Health Care Financing in Mainland Tanzania. 1975. 104 pp. $4.50.	Manuel Gottlieb
XXI.	Three Aspects of Crisis in Colonial Kenya. 1975. 91 pp & xxiii. $4.50.	Bismarck Myrick David L. Easterbrook Jack Roelker
XXII.	Africa and International Crises. 1976. 106 pp. $4.50.	Robert W. Brown Donald F. Heisel Charles H. Lyons Harvey Flad
XXIII.	Political Conflict and Ethnic Strategies: A Case Study of Burundi. 1976. 95 pp. $4.50.	Warren Weinstein Robert Schrire
XXIV.	Political Identity: A Case Study from Uganda. 1976. 185 pp. $5.50.	Marshall H. Segall Martin Doornbos Clive M. Davis
XXV.	East African Culture History. 1976. 93 pp. $4.50	Joseph T. Gallagher, Editor
XXVI.	Linguistic Diversity and Language Belief in Kenya: The Special Position of Swahili. 1977. 127 pp. $4.50.	John Rhoades
XXVII.	Exlorations in Quantitative African History. 1977. Approx 200 pp. $5.50	Joseph P. Smaldone, Editor
XXVIII.	Wildlife in Tanzanian Settlement Policy: The Case of the Selous. 1977. $5.50	Gordon Matzke
XXIX.	On His Majesty's Service: The Origin of Uganda's African Civil Service, 1912-1950. 1977. $4.50	Nizar Motani
XXX.	A Comparative Study of Political Involvement in Three African States: Botswana, Ghana and Kenya. 1977. $4.50	John D. Holm

EASTERN AFRICAN BIBLIOGRAPHIC SERIES

1. A Bibliography of Malawi. 1965. 161 pp. $5.00. — Edward F. Brown, Carol A. Fisher, John B. Webster

2. A Bibliography on Kenya. 1967. 461 pp. $8.00. — John B. Webster, Shirin G. Kassam, Robert S. Peckham, Barbara A. Skapa

3. The Guide to the Kenya National Archives. 1969. 452 pp. $13.00. — Robert G. Gregory, Robert Maxon

SPECIAL PUBLICATIONS

1. Basic Structure of Swahili. 1966. 151 pp. $3.50. — James L. Brain

2. Modern Makonde Sculpture Exhibit Catalogue. 1968. 103 pp. $4.00. — Aidron Duckworth

3. Shindano: Swahili Essays and Other Stories. 1971. 55 pp. $2.50. — Johannes C. Mlela, Jean F. O'Barr, Alice Grant, William O'Barr

OCCASIONAL BIBLIOGRAPHIES

18. A Guide to the Coast Province Microfilm Collection, Kenya National Archives. Kenya Seyidie (Coast) Province, Correspondence & Reports, 1891-1962. 1971. 191 pp. $4.50. — Harvey Soff

19. Microfilms Related to Eastern Africa, Part I (Kenya). A Guide to Recent Acquisitions of Syracuse University. 1971. 88 pp. $3.50. — R. F. Morton, Harvey Soff

20. A Supplement to a Select Bibliography of Soviet Publications on Africa. (1970-71). 1972. 27 pp. $2.50. — Ladislav Venys

21. Microfilms Related to Eastern Africa, Part II (Kenya, Asian and Miscellaneous). A Guide to Recent Acquisitions of Syracuse University. 1973. 142 pp. $4.50. — David Leigh, R. F. Morton

Occasional Bibliographies (Continued)

22. A Guide to the Nyanza Province Microfilm Collection, Kenya National Archives, Part I: Section 105B, Correspondence and Reports, 1925-1960. 1974. 137. $3.50. — Alan C. Solomon

23 A Select Bibliography of Soviet Publications on Africa in General and Eastern Africa in Particular. (1972-1973). 1974. 43 pp. $2.50 — Ladislav Venys

24. A Guide to the Nyanza Province Microfilm Collection, Kenya National Archives, Part II: Section 10A, Correspondence and Reports, 1899-1943. 1974. 50 pages. $3.50. — Alan C. Solomon

25. A Guide to Nyanza Province Microfilm Collections, Kenya National Archives, Part III: Section 10, Daily Correspondence and Reports, 1930-1963, Vol. I. 1975. 258 pp. & vi. $5.50. — Alan C. Solomon, Kenneth P. Lohrentz

26. A Guide to Nyanza Province Microfilm Collection, Kenya National Archives, Part III: Section 10, Daily Correspondence and Reports, 1930-1963, Vol. II. 1975. 254 pp. & vi. $5.50. — Kenneth P. Lohrentz, Alan C. Solomon

27. Microfilms Relating to Eastern Africa, Part III (Kenya and Miscellaneous): A Guide to Recent Acquisitions of Syracuse University. 1975. 112 pp. & iv. $4.50. — David L. Easterbrook, Alan C. Solomon

OCCASIONAL PAPERS

33. A Social Science Vocabulary of Swahili. 1968 43 pp. $2.50. — James L. Brain

50. Basic Structure of Swahili, Part II. 1969. 34 pp. $2.50. — James L. Brain

51. A Short Dictionary of Social Science Terms for Swahili Speakers. 1969. 70 pp. $3.50. — James L. Brain

Occasional Papers (Continued)

52. Environment Evaluation and Risk Adjustment in Eastern Africa. 1969. 53 pp. $4.50 — James L. Newman (Ed.)

53. The Pokot of Western Kenya 1910-1963: The Response of a Conservative People to Colonial Rule. 1969. 54 pp. $3.50. — L. D. Patterson

57. National Liberation and Culture (1970 Eduardo Mondlane Memorial Lecture). 1970. 15 pp. $3.00. — Amilcar Cabral

Publications may be ordered from:

Publications Desk
Foreign and Comparative Studies Program
119 College Place
Syracuse, N. Y. 13210

Maxwell School

Founded in 1924, the Maxwell School for fifty years has been training and educating young men and women for public service and academic careers. From the beginning the School has included all the University's social science departments, and this combination of professional and academic programs has enriched the content of all Maxwell's offerings. In addition to the traditional social science disciplines (Anthropology, Economics, Geography, History, Political Science, and Sociology), the School provides interdisciplinary degree programs in International Relations, Public Administration, the Social Sciences, and Urban and Regional Planning. Of the School's approximately 700 candidates for advanced degrees about half are in the traditional social science departments and the other half in interdisciplinary programs.

Today, the Maxwell School has 130 faculty members and approximately 700 students enrolled in graduate degree programs. Each year approximately 225 students receive master's degrees and 70 students Ph.D. degrees. In the three-year period, fall 1970 through spring 1973, Maxwell faculty members authored 78 books, 53 monographs, 296 articles, and 133 conference papers.